Historical Study

Former U.S. Bureau of Mines Property

Twin Cities Research Center

Prepared by:

Barbara J. Henning

Historian

RIVERCREST ASSOCIATES

203 North 13th Street
Petersburg, Illinois 62675
&

59 Monte Alto
Santa Fe, New Mexico 87505

Prepared for:

U.S. Department of the Interior

National Park Service

Final Report
October 2002

TABLE OF CONTENTS

Page

1. Introduction   1

Description of Project   1
    Scope of Work   1
    Boundaries   2
    Nomenclature   3
Previous Studies   3
    White and White   3
    Ollendorf and Godfrey   3
    Hotopp   4
    Clouse   4
Research Methods   5
End Notes   6

2. Context Statement   7

Introduction   7
Camp Coldwater Summer Camp   7
Settlers   8
Traders   9
    American Fur Company   9
    Benjamin F. Baker   10
Reserve Boundaries   11
    Camp Coldwater Residents   11
    Major Plympton Insists   12
St. Louis Hotel   13
Franklin Steele   15
George W. Lincoln   17
Conflict Near & Far   18
Department of the Dakota   19
Waterworks System   20
Coldwater Park   23
End of Federal Fort Snelling Era   23
Native Americans & Camp Coldwater   24
    Introduction   24
    Descriptions of the Area   24
    Encampments & Visits   25
    Summary   26
End Notes   27

3. Findings & Recommendations 31

Introduction 31
Significance of Coldwater Spring Site 31
Periods of Use 32
Government Use 33
Military 33
Entertainment/Recreation 34
Non-Government Use 34
Exploration/Settlement 34
Commerce 35

Integrity Matters 36
Archeological Remnants 36
Recommended Boundary Change 37
End Notes 37

Bibliography 38

Figures & Plates

Figure 1. Site Location.
Figure 2. Smith, E.K. Fort Snelling and Vicinity, October 1837.
Figure 3. R. Ames. Colby. Topographical View of a Portion of the Military Reserve, Embracing Fort Snelling. Ca. October and November 1839.
Figure 4. Fuller, George F. Plan of the Military Reserve at Fort Snelling Under the Direction of James W. Abert. Ca. 1853.
Figure 5. Map of the Military Reserve of Fort Snelling, Minnesota. Ca. 1870.

Figure 6. E.B. Summers. Map of Fort Snelling Reservation. 1882.
Figure 7. For Snelling Reservation. Ca. 1895-98. Copy from SHPO files
Figure 8. For Snelling Reservation. 1902. Copy from SHPO files.
Figure 9. W.H. Honnold, *et al.* Map of Fort Snelling and Vicinity. 1927. Copy made from Hotopp report.
Figure 10. Nyland, J.G. and A.J. Wattzelt. Fort Snelling Environs. 1934. Copy made from Hotopp report. Coldwater Park shown southeast of Veterans Hospital. Portion of larger map.

Figure 11. Fort Snelling National Historic Landmark Boundaries.
Figure 12. Fort Snelling National Register Historic District Boundaries.
Figure 13. Old Fort Snelling (State) Historic District Boundaries.
Figure 14. Recommended Boundary Changes Regarding Coldwater Spring Site at TCRC Property.
Figure 15. Proposed TCRC Historic District (Buildings).

PLATES

Plate 1. Coldwater reservoir and spring house with possible George Lincoln farmstead in background. Looking north. Ca. 1885. Source: MHS MH5.9/F1.3CW/r3.

Plate 2. Coldwater reservoir and spring house with pump house in background. Looking southwest. Ca. 1885. Source: MHS MH5.9/F1.3CW/r3.

Plate 3. Brick engineer's quarters built at the Coldwater Spring waterworks in 1899. Date of photograph not determined. Looking north? Source: MHS MSS 144.C.15.6(F).

Plate 4. Coldwater Spring waterworks, including engineer's quarters, pump house, reservoir, spring house, and two water tanks. 1905. Source: MHS MSS 144.C.15.6(F).

Plate 5. Aerial view of Coldwater Park. Ca. 1935. Source: MHS MH5.9/F1.3CW/p3.

ABSTRACT

The U.S. Bureau of Mines Twin Cities Research Center (TCRC), Main Campus, in Hennepin County, Minnesota closed in 1996. The National Park Service, which was assisting the Department of the Interior's Bureau of Mines Closure Team, became interested in obtaining well documented information to aid in determining appropriate future land use and management of the resources. The study involves focuses on the presence, significance, and integrity of historic resources on the TCRC property, especially those associated with Coldwater Spring. The area saw a number of uses associated with Fort Snelling beginning in 1820, including military, settlement, commercial, agricultural, public works, and recreational. The Coldwater Spring site is directly associated with important Fort Snelling activities. Due to these important associations, the Coldwater Spring site was included within the National Historic Landmark and National Register of Historic Places District, although the boundaries do not accurately represent this.

While demonstrably important to understanding Fort Snelling and environs history, the site does not appear to be individually eligible for listing in the National Register. The Coldwater Spring site draws its significance from its associations with the fort, as an important component of the compelling story of the fort and vicinity.

According to the National Historic Landmark nomination for Fort Snelling, it was "the first American fort in modern Minnesota" and was "of continuous significance in the security and development of the northwest region and in the transformation of the United States Army from a small frontier force to that of a major modern army." This historical study addresses this evolution in pages 6, 9-11, and 16-20. The rather brief NRHP nomination for Fort Snelling notes that the fort is significant in the areas of historic aboriginal presence, commerce, communications, military matters, political developments, transportation, and settlement of the frontier. While the focus of this historical study focuses on the uses of the area around the Coldwater Spring and the historic contexts specific to the area, the NRHP areas of significance are addressed on pages 6-23 of this report.

1. INTRODUCTION

DESCRIPTION OF THE PROJECT

Scope of Work

The Bureau of Mines, Twin Cities Research Center (TCRC), Main Campus property closed in 1996. Since that time, various agencies have grappled with what the most appropriate use or uses of the property might be. In January 2002, the U.S. Fish and Wildlife Service assumed management responsibility of the property.

The primary objective of the study is to provide well documented information to the National Park Service and other interested agencies and parties to aid in determining appropriate future land use and management of the resources. In particular, the presence or absence of significant resources, that is, resources that might be individually eligible for the National Register of Historic Places or might contribute to the significance of an historic district or national landmark designation, is an important part of this historical study.

A secondary objective is to provide information that might be applied to the proper interpretation of the Bureau of Mines TCRC Main Campus between the years 1820, when the first known use of the property occurred, and 1946, when the Veterans Administration assumed responsibility for the property, thereby ending its formal association with Fort Snelling. Such information could be used to generate exhibits and publications to inform the public.

More specifically, the scope of work for this historical study listed several areas to address. We were asked to determine how the federal government used the TCRC Main Campus property between 1820 and 1946, identifying key phases of government use in the process. Part of that identification involved determining buildings that had been present, what types of activities took place, and whether potential historic resources still existed. In addition to governmental uses, non-governmental uses on the TCRC Main Campus were to be determined and researched. Since considerable research and writing has been completed on the years from 1820 to 1837, under the scope of work, we focused on the years 1838 to 1946 in conducting the research. Similarly, a recent investigation (discussed below) covered the history of the TCRC after 1946, eliminating the need for additional study of the post-1946 period.

While it would have been useful to pinpoint the locations of the many buildings, structures, and objects in the study area, the type and quality of maps, iconography, and other documentation was too vague and, in some cases, contradictory to allow for meaningful placement of historic structures or features on current maps.

Another group of users on the TCRC Main Campus property, Native Americans, was also to be researched, including discussion of the earliest written references through 1946. This historical study is not a Traditional Cultural Property (TCP) assessment. Since we were already studying the historical record to prepare a history of the property between 1820 and 1946, it seemed appropriate to include references encountered in the course of research to Native American uses of the TCRC Main Campus property.

Based on the history of the TCRC Main Campus property, we were to determine whether the boundaries of the National Historic Landmark (NHL) or the Fort Snelling National Register of Historic Places District should be amended to more appropriately reflect the elements that contribute to the significance of both the NHL and the National Register District. (We believe the boundary descriptions of the nominations should be expanded to include the Coldwater Spring environs.) It is beyond the scope of work to address whether the NHL boundary should include the National Register district beyond the TCRC property and the relationship with the Old Fort Snelling district.

Boundaries

Located near the confluence of the Minnesota and Mississippi rivers, the study area is located in or near a number of governmental designations, a reflection of the longstanding historic and geographic importance of the immediate area. The property is within the boundary of the Mississippi National River and Recreation Area, a unit of the National Park System. A portion of the Bureau of Mines property lies within the Fort Snelling National Historic Landmark and also within part of the Fort Snelling National Register of Historic Places District. It should be noted that because these listings occurred during the fledgling years of the National Register and Historic Landmark programs when guidelines were not available, the landmark and the district have slightly different boundaries. (Figures 11. and 12.)

The Minnesota SHPO has also determined that most of the buildings on the TCRC Main Campus are eligible for the National Register as a district, based on a report by Anthony Godfrey. Godfrey's work eliminated the need to expand our study beyond 1946. Significant between 1949 and 1993, the proposed district is a

> "classic" representation of a modern government scientific research center based on bureaucratic knowledge production. The Twin Cities Research Center typified this 1950s trend toward Big Science, which grew in [the?] decade whereby Americans had an almost "cult-like" faith in science to solve the world's problems.[1]

Furthermore, the proposed TCRC historic district is considered significant for the property's contribution to and direct association with the science and technology of mineral production and mining, especially the development of the Tilden iron ore processing of nonmagnetic taconite.

Portions of the area have also received State of Minnesota recognition. The state-listed Old Fort Snelling Historic District is adjacent to the TCRC Main Campus property, and the National Register-listed Minnehaha Historic District is also nearby. Figures 11-13 and 15 show current boundaries for the Fort Snelling National Historic Landmark, the Fort Snelling National Register Historic District, the state Old Fort Snelling Historic District, and the proposed TCRC Historic District.

Nomenclature

Located on the Upper Bluff area and distinct from Fort Snelling the study area includes Coldwater Spring. The many layers of history represented have direct associations with the spring. Between 1820 and 1946, the study area was the site of Camp Coldwater, the Baker trading post and associated non-federal settlement, the Coldwater waterworks for Fort Snelling, and Coldwater Park. Because of these historical associations with Coldwater Spring, the study area will be referred to in this report with respect to the Coldwater Spring rather than the later, post-1946 Bureau of Mines TCRC period.

PREVIOUS STUDIES

White and White Ethnographic & Historical Study

A number of studies have dealt directly with the Coldwater Spring area. Helen White and Bruce White's *Fort Snelling in 1838: An Ethnographic and Historical Study* is a detailed, well researched look at the fort and environs at a specific point in time. Their contention that it is vital to look beyond the military personnel and function of the fort is entirely appropriate and was applied to this study. Applying the important work of White and White as a springboard for additional research, we examined the roles of fur traders, civilians, Native Americans, excursionists, and farmers in connection with the Coldwater Spring vicinity. The White and White report provided useful, new information on Benjamin F. Baker as well as beginning the process of compiling data on Camp Coldwater early occupants.[2]

Ollendorf and Godfrey Archeological & Historical Study

With the decision to end federal funding of the U.S. Bureau of Mines in 1996, it was necessary to conduct archeological and historical studies of the Twin Cities Research Center (TCRC) campus as part of the process of closing the facility. The TCRC buildings were found to be eligible for listing in the National Register as an historic district of 13 contributing buildings and structures and two non-contributing buildings. The district was deemed NRHP-eligible because it represented "a significant national and regional element in the history of science and technology of mineral production and mining for the time period 1949 to 1996."[3]

The archeological study conducted in 1996 involved both assessing the presence or absence of potentially significant resources (Phase I survey) and also determining the NRHP-eligibility of located resources (Phase II investigation). The report concluded that none of the features and artifacts encountered were significant based on National Register guidelines.

Hotopp Trunk Highway 55 Archeological Study

Because the Minnesota Department of Transportation was planning to reroute State Trunk Highway 55 in an area once associated with Camp Coldwater, the highway department conducted a study of the route's potential impact to cultural resources. The planned route (which has since been completed) when through portions of the historic Camp Coldwater area (north of the spring and not on TCRC property) and threatened four burr oak trees some considered culturally important. The Hotopp report discussed in considerable detail ethnohistoric accounts of Dakota sacred places, especially around Fort Snelling, and provided a wealth of maps and historic photographs illustrating the subject area. Information concerning the significance of springs and also maps the Hotopp researchers obtained from the National Archives were applied to this report. Hotopp concluded that there was little likelihood that prehistoric graves would occur near the four oaks and that the trees were not eligible for the National Register due to the lack of documentation supporting their possible historic significance. The report also stated that the Coldwater Spring area should be considered a contributing element to the Fort Snelling Historic District and that there was insufficient information or documentation to assess the area's standing as a Traditional Cultural Property.[4]

Clouse Archeological Study

As part of the TCRC closure process, the National Park Service and the Minnesota Historical Society decided to conduct a joint archeological study of the TCRC property. Robert A. Clouse of the Minnesota Historical Society (MHS) was selected to conduct the study. Clouse, who has since left MHS, has studied Fort Snelling for decades, and the fort was the subject of his dissertation.

Digging some 30 test units, Clouse found no evidence of prehistoric use of the Coldwater Spring area, although he noted that the area was likely used by Native Americans. Despite the many changes to the land forms and the presence of wet areas, Clouse located some historic materials, many if not most from the second half of the 19th century. A bone comb fragment and an English style gunflint found in his Zone II dated from the early 19th century.

Based on his field investigations, Clouse concluded that one large area (Zone II, generally west of the spring) contained "in situ cultural deposits and buried soils as well as material culture dating to the period of significance of the NHL and NR District."

Another area required additional testing in his estimation, while still other management zones did not contain "cultural resources contributing to the significance of the NHL." Some portions of the study area, including the Coldwater Spring reservoir, were not included in the zones Clouse devised.[5]

It should be noted that Clouse found early historic materials under considerable fill. It appears that the earlier Ollendorf study failed to find significant cultural resources of this sort because they did not get through the thick fill layer in their excavations. Changes in landform during construction of the TCRC, in effect, protected some of the early deposits while also obscuring them from the Ollendorf crew.

RESEARCH METHODS

The Scope of Work for this project rightly noted that considerable research has been conducted regarding Coldwater Spring and environs for the period 1820 through 1837. Therefore, we drew upon this body of research and concentrated on events from 1838 to 1946. The majority of the research was conducted using Minnesota Historical Society holdings and Rivercrest Associates research materials. The following are the principal resources consulted for the project:

    --Historic maps
    --Historic photographs
    --Official records for Fort Snelling, including building records, special orders, correspondence
    --Contemporary accounts and reminiscences
    --1998 report by White and White
    --Census data (for George Lincoln family)
    --Statewide histories, especially the work of Folwell
    --Hennepin County histories
    --Previous studies discussed above

Historic contexts and related property types are a useful framework for researching and evaluating a particular place. "Theme, place, and time are the basic elements that define historic contexts."[6] We concentrated on those contexts that illuminated the Camp Coldwater area rather than at times outdated, previously identified Fort Snelling historic themes found in the NHL and NRHP nominations. Nonetheless, we believe our contexts and property types tie into previous investigations.

These three variables—the what, where, and when—of the historic context are clearly part of both the natural and cultural environments. A cultural evolutionary and ecological orientation assumes that human activities are directly affected by the environment and that those activities can be traced, more or less, through time. When researching past human activity, we define a natural environment and a cultural environment. Both environments in combination affected a given population at any given point in time.

The development of appropriate historic contexts provides a valuable tool for understanding the importance and evolution of a study area and for evaluating the significance of particular properties and sites. Based on research into a variety of topics, the contexts and property types which define the area are identified. We view the historical development of the overall region, the locality, and specific properties within these contexts. Broad contexts are applied to a specific area's settlement and land use history.

---

[1] Amy Ollendorf, *Twin Cities Research Center, U.S. Bureau of Mines*, Final Report, 1996, p. 6. Anthony Godfrey conducted the historical portion of the report.

[2] Helen White and Bruce White, *Fort Snelling in 1838: An Ethnographic and Historical Study*. Report prepared for Minnesota Historical Society, 1998.

[3] Amy Ollendorf, *Twin Cities Research Center, U.S. Bureau of Mines*, Final Report, 1996, p. 1B-3 (quoting). Anthony Godfrey conducted the historical portion of the report.

[4] John A. Hotopp, *et al.*, *A Cultural Resource Assessment of the Proposed Reroute for Trunk Highway 55, 54th Street to County, Road 62, Hennepin County, Minnesota*. Report prepared for the Federal Highway Administration and MnDOT. 1999, see especially pp. 50-56, 59-61.

[5] Robert Clouse, *Archaeological Research at the former Twin Cities Bureau of Mines Testing Facility, Minnesota*. Prepared for the National Park Service. Draft report, August 2001, *passim* and p. 87, quoting.

[6] U.S. Department of the Interior, *National Register Bulletin 16. Guidelines for Completing National Register of Historic Places Forms*. 1986, p. 7.

2. Context Statement

INTRODUCTION

U.S. military officials established what became known as Fort Snelling at the confluence of two major waterways, the Mississippi and Minnesota (originally St. Peters) rivers. The site was chosen based on its strategic location at the rivers, its location between Dakota and Chippewa lands, and its placement below the Falls of St. Anthony, an impediment to steamboat navigation. Prior to construction of railroads in the area, the fort was situated to be able to control Native American movement, trade, commerce, and Euro-American settlement over a vast area.

The establishment of a fort in the developing frontier typically occasioned the arrival of persons officially and unofficially associated with the fort. Fort Snelling was no exception to this pattern, and an Indian Agency (established the summer of 1820 by Lawrence Taliaferro), fur trading operations (including the American Fur Company established in 1821 at Mendota), missionaries, and settlers with various motives and inclinations at one time or another could be found near the fort, including examples at Coldwater Spring. (Figure 3. shows the major land uses present in the Fort Snelling environs in the early 19th century.)

The Coldwater Spring environs is directly associated with the initial Euro-American settlement of the Twin Cities area. It was a locus for nonmilitary activities, ones prominently associated with the founding years of Minnesota. Early residents evicted in 1840 settled up portions of St. Paul while others remained in the Minneapolis area to provide the foundation for permanent settlement there. While Stillwater lays claim to be the birthplace of Minnesota on political grounds, the Coldwater Spring area can rightly be seen as the beginnings of permanent settlement in the Twin Cities. It holds a unique place in the history of the state.

The focus of this study is the area known as Camp Coldwater or Coldwater Spring, which is located within the confines of the Twin Cities Research Center Main Campus. The activities of the various occupants of the area around Fort Snelling will be discussed primarily as they relate to Camp Coldwater. (It should be noted that a previous study by Ollendorf and Godfrey determined that the TCRC Main Campus is eligible for listing in the NRHP, and the Minnesota State Historic Preservation Officer agreed. Because of this previous study, we did not look beyond the close of military ownership in 1946.)

CAMP COLDWATER SUMMER CAMP

Arriving late in the summer of 1819, Lieutenant Colonel Henry Leavenworth led a contingent of approximately 200 soldiers of the U.S. Army to the Fort Snelling site. They established a temporary facility on the south side of the Minnesota River, which they named New Hope, and spent the winter of 1819-20 encamped there. The site was considered undesirable for summertime residency—Indian trader Philander Prescott characterized the area as "flats and swamps" come summer—and Leavenworth directed that they move to a new location. Intended as a temporary expedient, the summer camp was located at Coldwater Spring on the west bank of the Mississippi River and north of the present site of Fort Snelling. The presence of a clear and flowing spring was undoubtedly a factor in site selection. The establishment of the summer camp is the first documented use of the Camp Coldwater area. Prescott noted that the military spent the next summer (1820) setting up the new camp and preparing gardens.[1]

Before Leavenworth could commence building a permanent fort, he was transferred, and Colonel Josiah Snelling stepped in to direct construction of the fort that was eventually named after him. In the course of construction, soldiers used Camp Coldwater as a base of operations during the summer. Camp Coldwater functioned as a military cantonment perhaps as much as the summers of 1820, 1821, and 1822, and perhaps longer but in diminishing degrees.

Sources vary for the date of the fort's completion or occupation, with 1821, 1822, 1823, and 1824 mentioned. Noted historian, William Watts Folwell, has noted that contemporaries present during construction gave differing years for when the fort was first occupied. Some were evidently referring to the date the fort was initially occupied, while others are discussing the date of construction completion. Historian Theodore Blegan concludes that "by the summer of 1824 the colonel [Snelling] was able to report that that year would witness the completion of the fort." General Winfield Scott inspected the post in 1824 and was pleased by its appearance. An 1881 Hennepin County history states that the fort was "first occupied in October, 1822." Philander Prescott recalled that most soldiers were living there by the autumn of 1823, whereas Charlotte O. Van Cleve, who came to the fort as a newborn and later wrote a book about the fort, thought they had moved into the partially completed fort in 1821.[2]

While the exact date of completion is debatable, it appears likely that some military personnel moved to the new fort as soon as there were buildings ready to accommodate them. Probably during the winter of 1822-23, construction was sufficiently along to provide shelter for some or all of the troops. It seems unlikely that any troops lived near Coldwater Spring during the summers after construction on the permanent fort was well underway; however, it is possible that for some reason it was more efficient for them to continue to occupy the area in the summer. The Camp Coldwater period, 1820 to 1822 or 1823, was the first nonfederal use of the study area.[3]

SETTLERS

The Selkirk agricultural colony, a group the Scottish Earl of Selkirk sponsored and encouraged to settle in the Red River area far northwest of Fort Snelling beginning in 1811, was one source of settlers who gravitated to the fort. It appears the first group arrived in 1821. Intense conflict with fur trading interests and their French-Indian representatives as well as the rigors of isolated frontier living propelled the immigrants from the Red River region. Alexis Bailly, then agent of the American Fur Company with headquarters at Mendota, obtained a contract to provide cattle to the Selkirk colony. Using the Red River trail, he drove a herd to the colony and sold them. It is reported that five Swiss families returned with Bailly to Fort Snelling where they were permitted to remain. The exact location these squatters chose is not known, save that it was "near Fort Snelling." It would have been reasonable for them to choose a site near a good water source, such as Coldwater Spring.[4]

As conditions at the Selkirk colony become increasingly perilous, more and more families left and came to Fort Snelling. For example, 13 Swiss families came to the fort in 1823. Their arrival did not go unnoticed. Trader Benjamin F. Baker complained to Indian Agent Taliaferro that "these people that come from Red River have lodged about a hundred head of Cattle in the Bottom where we had inclosed [sic] for our Stock and they are destroying the Pasture." Some remained in the vicinity for some time, then moved on, while others remained until forced to leave.[5] Since Baker's trading house was located by the Coldwater Spring, it is possible he was referring to land in the general Camp Coldwater area.

Many others from the beleaguered Selkirk colony sought refuge at the fort, including a party of 243 in 1826. Most left the immediate fort area, but "a number of farms were opened on the military tract in 1827," and the settlers remained there until the 1838 ratification of the treaty of 1837.[6]

In addition to the Selkirk colony refugees, other settlers could be found in the Fort Snelling environs in the 1830s. It appears that most of them either had an association with fur traders, were employed by the Indian Agency or the fort, or a combination of these activities. These settlers also typically engaged in some sort of farming, but they are discussed in below.

TRADERS

American Fur Company

As noted previously, Alexis Bailly arrived in 1821 and set up the American Fur Company headquarters near the New Hope site in present Mendota. The fur company was located south of Camp Coldwater and Fort Snelling on the south bank of the Minnesota River. In 1834, Henry Hastings Sibley arrived to take over the American Fur Company presence in the Snelling environs. In 1835, he built a fine stone house that functioned as headquarters for the business. The American Fur Company was the major fur trading operation in the area, and various settlers and workers could be found in and around it.[7] The area at the confluence of the Minnesota and Mississippi rivers was a locus for pre-territorial activities. The Indian Agency, fur trading establishment, and the fort fulfilled important roles in an era when the fur trade was an important economic venture that had profound effects on the region.

Benjamin F. Baker

Another important early trader ran an independent operation. Benjamin Baker (the complainer about Selkirk colony cattle in 1823) had received licenses to trade with the Native Americans from the Indian Agent in 1833 and 1834 from his Coldwater Spring facility (and probably for other years in other locations). Around 1837, he built a prominent stone trading house by Coldwater Spring. The desire to have a stone building may have been evidence of competition with the American Fur Company in nearby Mendota.[8] (See Figures 2. and 3.)

Baker was an important figure in the Camp Coldwater story, and his various activities illustrate the types of nonmilitary endeavors present during the pioneer period in Minnesota. Born in Virginia in 1800, by 1823 Baker was at Fort Snelling, having originally come to teach the children associated with the fort. However, he soon abandoned that activity and embarked on the fur trading career. Baker headed north into Ojibwe country and had posts at several spots, including Leech Lake and Crow Wing, the latter on the Mississippi River. He married a part-Ojibwe woman with whom he had five children.

After a Dakota attack on his Crow Wing post in 1832, Baker withdrew and established his trading operation at Coldwater Spring. His business was sufficient to require employees, including Martin McLeod, Jesse Taylor and Joseph Robinette. (Ever energetic, Baker and McLeod established a short-lived school at Camp Coldwater the winter of 1837-8.)

The fur trading business was not thriving, suffering from low prices in the 1836-37 season. Baker's precarious financial situation may have propelled him into different economic pursuits. Philander Prescott reportedly bought out Baker and spent the summer of 1838 and the winter of 1838-39 at the trading post (Camp Coldwater) where he "made a little trade."[9]

Baker turned to the developing lumber industry centered in the St. Croix Valley. He sent employees there to stake claims, planned a saw mill, and sought equipment from St. Louis. (Popular and well-connected with fort officers and fellow Virginian, Indian Agent Taliaferro, Baker was also appointed acting post sutler in the late 1830s.) Needing assistance from creditors in St. Louis, Baker went there in 1839. He was suffering from tuberculosis, and died. Prior to Baker's death, longtime friend Kenneth McKenzie provided some funding, then acted as Baker's agent clearing up the tangled business affairs, a project that persisted into the 1850s. Following Benjamin Baker's demise at age 39, the stone trading house he constructed was host to a variety of users (discussed below).[10]

The fur trade era at Camp Coldwater was of relatively brief duration, dating from around 1833 until 1840 when Major Plympton directed the removal of all settlers at Camp Coldwater. However, it was an integral part of a larger and more longstanding effort to exploit Minnesota natural resources. The fur trade marked the initial European presence in the region and heralded profound changes regarding who occupied the land and how natural resources were perceived and used.

RESERVE BOUNDARIES

Major Joseph Plympton assumed command of Fort Snelling the summer of 1837. He ordered census of the area and a survey of the fort environs showing the current conditions. The major was interested in determining the correct and appropriate boundaries for the military reservation. In addition, he was concerned about the rapidly diminishing presence of nearby timber for fuel and building purposes, the presence of illegal settlers on federal land, and the growing number of establishments selling liquor to Native Americans and soldiers.

Lt. E. K. Smith completed mapping and census taking in 1837. (Figure 2.) He reported to Plympton:

> The white inhabitants in the vicinity of the fort, as near as I could ascertain, are: 82 in Baker's settlement, around old Camp Coldwater, and at Massey's landing. On the other side, 25 at the fur company's establishment, including Terrebault's [Faribault's] and Le Clerc's [LeClaire's], 50. Making a total of 157 souls in no way connected with the military.[11]

Camp Coldwater Residents

The map Lt. Smith prepared reveals those residences and workplaces by name present in October of 1837 at Camp Coldwater. A number of sources from the 1830s provide information about who lived in and around Camp Coldwater, including the census of 1838. Nine Fort Snelling area residents signed a petition dated August 16, 1837 in which they claimed they had all "erected houses and cultivated fields" in the confines of the military reserve and that none were Indian traders. Research by local historians has uncovered additional information about the 1830s Camp Coldwater residents.[12]

-- Jacobs or Jacob. Engaged in blacksmithing. Jacob is not represented in the 1838 census.
-- Oliver Cratt or Cratte. He was a blacksmith for the Indian Agency and had a stable at his Camp Coldwater place of residence. In 1838 there were three males and four females in the home. He was among those who signed the 1837 petition. The family appears in the Loras 1839 baptismal register.

-- Peter Quin or Quinn. He served as an interpreter for the Indian Agency. The 1838 census found three males four females. Quin also signed the 1837 petition, and was Catholic, appearing in the Loras 1839 register. There may have been a stable on his piece of land near the Coldwater Spring. Born in Ireland, he came to Fort Snelling in 1823 and worked for many years as a trader and Ojibwe interpreter.

-- Louis Buisson. In 1838 the household consisted of two males and two females. He signed the petition as a settler and apparently had a fenced field or other enclosure.

-- Antoine Pepin or Papin. Pepin was another Indian Agency blacksmith. According to the 1838 census there were nine males and three females present. Pepin signed the 1837 petition. He came to the Fort Snelling area in June 1832 from Red River. He was appointed blacksmith to the Dakota and repaired their traps. In 1836 Oliver Cratte replaced him because he could also repair guns. Pepin moved to St. Paul in 1843.

-- Le Rage or Joseph Reche or Resch. It appears that La Rage and Joseph Reche are the same person, but this has not been determined with certainty. Joseph Reshe was at some point an Indian Agency blacksmith's assistant. The 1838 census showed seven males and three females in the household. He signed the 1837 petition and is present in the Loras 1839 register.

-- Benjamin F. Baker. According to Smith's 1837 map, Baker's trading post included five or six buildings. He would have needed adequate space to accommodate the 12 males and three females in residence in 1838.

Additional settlers were located below Camp Coldwater along the river (and outside the study area. In 1837, these consisted of the households of Abraham Perry (by the steamboat landing), Louis Massy, and Louis Brunnel. Six other households were in residence across the Mississippi River from Camp Coldwater.

While Lt. Smith found 82 residents situated in the Camp Coldwater area, including Massey's landing, census figures from 1838 show 55 in the immediate Coldwater area, and a dozen more in the Massy and Brunnel households, for a total of 67. There were seven households and some 20 buildings in the immediate Camp Coldwater area.

Major Plympton Insists

On July 26, 1838, Major Plympton announced that further building or timber cutting was not acceptable. The directive was intended to encourage the squatters or illegal settlers to vacate the area. The following spring, Plympton felt further or renewed concern about all the groggeries on east side of the Mississippi. To limit their presence, he recommended removal of all "white intruders" on the public lands within 20 miles of the fort.[13]

The federal government sometimes moves slowly, and it was another year before the final directive was put into play. In May of 1840, the U.S. Marshall from Wisconsin Territory received formal authority to remove all illegal settlers and to use Fort Snelling troops if necessary. And it was necessary. On May 6, 1840, soldiers removed people and reportedly destroyed their log cabins.[14] With the enforced removal of illegal settlers from the Camp Coldwater area, a third phase of land use developed.

ST. LOUIS HOTEL

After Major Plympton caused the removal of those who had illegally settled within the Fort Snelling reserve, at least one nonmilitary use at Camp Coldwater persisted. Although the trader Benjamin F. Baker had died in St. Louis in 1839, his large stone trading house was put to an alternate use, as the St. Louis Hotel, and also, for a time, a fur trading enterprise also persisted at the property. It appears that Fort Snelling officials continued to allow certain nonfederal use of the Camp Coldwater area, just as they had in the early 1830s when Baker had licenses to trade with the Indians there.

In 1841 two traders, Martin McLeod and Norman Kittson, were located at Camp Coldwater when Eli Pettijohn came to the area on April 16, 1841. He found McLeod (along with his infant son Walter) occupying the former Baker trading house which was located "near where the water tower now stands" [ca. 1914]. Kittson "lived at his trading post about 50 yards away from the [Baker] house," suggesting that not all log cabins were razed in 1840. Kittson was in residence temporarily or intermittently, for from 1842-44 he operated a trading post in Baytown on the St. Croix. It appears that both the stone trading house (later known as the St. Louis Hotel), and at least one log cabin still stood in 1840.[15]

When Pettijohn inquired of a place to stay, he was directed to the "St. Louis house," formerly Baker's ca. 1837 stone trading house. After Baker died in 1839 and with the enforced removal of illegal settlers in 1840, the building stood essentially vacant and available for any travelers or others in need of accommodation to use. For example, in 1840 and 1841, the Gideon and Samuel Pond families, missionaries to the Dakota, took up residence for several years after they were told to re-locate from Lake Harriet, to either Traverse des Sioux or Lake Traverse. Both of the Pond brothers refused this directive out of concerns for the safety their families and lived at the Baker trading house until they secure permanent accommodation outside the Fort Snellings environs.[16]

Some time after 1841, McLeod abandoned the Baker house. After being abandoned for a short time, by 1853 the house was refurbished into a hotel for the growing tourist business on the upper Mississippi River.

Beginning in the late 1830s and with growing enthusiasm in the succeeding two decades, increasing numbers of tourists took steamboats up the Mississippi to see the wonderful scenery in and around Fort Snelling, which provided a new use for the Baker house. The artist George Catlin was among the first to promote the area. Later artists also spread the word, adding to interest in the upper Mississippi River as a tourist destination. One effective artistic technique was the preparation of immense panoramas depicting the upper Mississippi region. The artist Henry Lewis toured the country in 1848 with a rolled canvas that was 1200 yards long and twelve feet high.[17]

Other visitors wrote of their trip to Minnesota. In a book published in 1853, Mrs. Elizabeth Ellet listed the places she toured around Fort Snelling. By stagecoach she went from St. Paul to the falls of St. Anthony, then to lakes Harriett and Calhoun, Minnehaha Falls, Fort Snelling, and past the Spring Cave when returning to St. Paul. She did not mention Coldwater Spring or the St. Louis Hotel.[18] Another female writer, Harriet Bishop, did comment on the St. Louis Hotel in a work published in 1857. "The St. Louis House is on our way [from Minnehaha to the fort]. Until recently it was a dilapidated mass of stone and mortar….Enlarged and improved, it is now a delightful summer resort for southerners and a great convenience to the excursionist."[19]

The conversion from trading post to hotel is depicted on historic maps. Two maps from the 1850s variously showed a "Hotel" near Cold Spring or just a building symbol. The old stone trading post and later hotel was still in use in 1853, the approximate date of one of the maps, and remained in good condition as late as 1857.[20] (Figure 4.)

Between the summer of 1858 and 1862, the John Chapin family operated the St. Louis Hotel primarily as a boarding house. Two of Chapin's granddaughters, Mary Mead Moffett and Elva Mead Knotts, and Harriet Godfrey whose family operated a nearby saw mill recalled the hotel some 70 years later. Godfrey was able to draw upon her mother's diary which noted on June 18, 1858, that "Men at the mill going to board at the St. Louis House."[21]

Writing in 1930, Moffett and Knotts thought as many as 80 boarders at one time lived there, many of whom worked at a nearby mill (probably on Minnehaha Creek). Chapin's granddaughters recalled that John Chapin's daughter Marie married Leander A. Dow at the St. Louis House, and their son Johnnie may have been born at the hotel as well. One of the children of another aunt, Augusta Chapin Harris, was also said to have been born at the hotel.[22]

Also writing in 1930 (and corresponding with Moffett and Knotts), Harriet Godfrey described the former trading house turned hotel. It had a "long wooden ell or wing extending to the south much larger than the front and I believe painted white." And "the spring was down a slight declevity [declivity] on the north side of the house toward the river, beautiful, clear, cold water, that neighbors took away by the barrel in their wagons." Below the lofty hotel site was a ferry landing.

Mary Moffett described in detail the furnishings and interior of St. Louis House, but it is not clear how accurate her recollections were given the amount of time that had passed.

> Mother said there were three parts to the "Old St. Louis House." One part was frame, one part brick and one was stone. The rooms were large. The dining room had lovely black walnut tables and chairs, very large sideboards with several candelabras for the table, also candlesticks in sliver [silver]. The china was the best and complete for the tables, silver service

for the tables; also 3 sizes of goblets, the smaller one for wine. I
remember mother telling about individual egg cups.

There was a very large sitting room, a large parlor with French windows.
These rooms had velvet carpets, mahogany furniture upholstered in black
hair-cloth and some in red plush, several settees, and marble-top tables.
These rooms had large chandeliers also in the dining room, which hung in
the center. The bed rooms were furnished in black walnut, marble-top
bureau[s] and plint [plinth?] bottom chairs, wash bowl and pitcher for each
bed room; split bottom rocking chairs for the bedrooms.[23]

It is difficult to imagine workmen from the saw mill in such a fine setting. No other
mention of a brick portion of the hotel has come to light.

The St. Louis House burned in 1862. The Chapin grandchildren were presumably able to
recall the date of the fire, the spring of 1862, because the family moved to the open land
around 31 miles from Fort Ridgley. They were in residence there when the conflict with
the Sioux erupted in August of 1862 and the family quickly headed back to the Fort
Snelling environs. That the St. Louis House was able to operate and thrive was probably
the result of Franklin Steele's efforts to purchase the Fort Snelling military reserve.

FRANKLIN STEELE

As the line of frontier settlement moved away from Fort Snelling, new forts were
constructed in Minnesota, including Fort Ridgely in 1854 and Fort Abercrombie in 1857.
The Army reduced the number of troops at the fort, and it devolved into a rather
awkwardly located supply depot of sorts with limited personnel. Ever mindful of ways to
economize, Congress and the U.S. military considered the military or strategic import of
the numerous forts established across the country. As the frontier moved westward, some
forts in their wake were considered unnecessary and no longer of value to the federal
government.[24]

Fort Snelling was among those early forts whose utility was questioned. The military
reserve comprised twelve square miles in a rapidly developing area. A mere forty acres
was considered more than adequate for the fort, now considered primarily a supply
depot.[25]

Federal officials took steps to dispose of the excess land. Two commissioners were
selected, Major Seth Eastman and William King Heiskell. The pair determined that the
reserve should be sold for $90,000 as a single unit and under a private sale. Further,
ostensibly because Franklin Steele had (with permission) built a house, storehouse, and
outbuildings on fort land, the commissioners determined that he merited the right of first
refusal. A Minnesota resident since 1837, Steele had served as post sutler. The
commissioners made their offer to Steele, and on June 8, 1857, he agreed to buy nearly
8,000 acres for $90,000.[26]

As part of the negotiations for the sale of the Fort Snelling reserve in 1857, Eastman and Heiskell prepared a report dated June 10, 1857. They found the following notable private property located within the reserve:

> There is a large and valuable stone building with a frame addition, making an extensive house, which has been furnished and used as a hotel, which could not have cost less that $15,000. The stone part was built in 1837, by a Mr. Baker, afterwards sutler at Fort Snelling. It was sold to Kenneth McKenzie, esq., who, in 1853, put on the extensive addition alluded to, put the entire building in good order, and furnished it for a house of accommodation. Mr. Steele having arranged with Mr. Kenneth McKenzie for this property, and secured the government from all claims from this source, we are positive, therefore, in saying that Mr. Steele is the only claimant to the improvements upon the same [hotel] made by citizens.[27]

Kenneth McKenzie of St. Louis was a long time friend of Benjamin Baker. In fact, when Baker was dying he asked McKenzie to take care of his business affairs, a rather complicated tangle of fur shipments, land claims, and sutler accounts whose disposition persisted into the 1850s.[28] It is possible that McKenzie did not own the hotel himself but, in his capacity as handler of Baker's affairs (who died in 1839), he chose to improve the building to make it more valuable to the Baker estate.

McKenzie must have welcomed the assessment that the hotel was worth $15,000. On June 9, 1857, when negotiations were underway between Steele and the federal government, Henry M. Rice, prominent Minnesota politician and former partner with Henry Sibley in fur trade ventures, acted as his attorney in fact for McKenzie. Rice was able to obtain $15,000 from Franklin Steele for the Baker house and the quarter section of land around it. This payment to McKenzie cleared up the possibility of competing claims for the military reserve, and Steele became the owner of the Fort Snelling reserve, effective July 2, 1857.[29]

Steele made an initial payment of $30,000 for the Fort Snelling reserve and prepared to plat, sell, and otherwise develop the property. The circumstances behind the sale, why Steele was so readily selected to be the buyer, and the possible involvement of land speculators was cause for Congressional study in later years.

In the 1850s, Minnesota (and other Midwest areas) was experiencing a land boom of unprecedented proportions. Speculators flocked to the region. The prices for land, lots, and property skyrocketed. To take advantage of the demand for property in the Minneapolis and St. Paul vicinity, Steele had the City of Fort Snelling platted in 1857. The boom did not last, and beginning in August of 1857, just a month after the sale of the reserve, the nationwide Financial Panic of 1857 began.[30]

The financial ruin rippled across the country. Banks closed, ambitious plans ceased, commerce slowed to a trickle. Mr. I.A. Pelton, who came to Minnesota in April 1858, recalled that "Everyone was badly in debt and money was hard to get. Currency consisted of old guns, town lots, basswood lumber, etc. These things were traded for goods and groceries." Under these circumstances, Steele was unable to make either of the two additional payments when they came due.[31]

While Steele was the titular owner of the former Fort Snelling reserve, a route for the Minnesota & Cedar Valley Railroad was graded through the Camp Coldwater area east of the spring. The M & CV Railroad was among the first important land grant railroads in the state. After the Civil War, in 1865, the Chicago Milwaukee & St. Paul Railroad was built on the 1858 grade, another nonfederal use of the Camp Coldwater vicinity. (As part of construction of the post's modern waterworks system at Coldwater Spring in the 1880s and 1890s, a spur line was built from the venerable rail route to the new waterworks.)

GEORGE W. LINCOLN

Private use of the Coldwater Spring area was not confined to the early fur trading years. During the period when Franklin Steele sought Fort Snelling, the George Lincoln family was an occupant of the area.

In 1857, George Lincoln or Lincolin, who was born in Maine, resided at St. Anthony in Hennepin County, Minnesota. He was then 22 years old and working as a teamster. Lincoln evidently resided in a boarding house of some sort, for 16 other men and three women were also in residence. Lincoln may have deemed it advisable to leave his native state, for in 1854, one George W. Lincoln owed a debt that was brought to the attention of the courts in Kennebec County, Maine.[32]

Lincoln may have learned of the opportunities manifest in the Fort Snelling area from a fellow Maine resident. James A. Dunsmoor was from Harmony, Maine, which is in or near present Kennebec County. Dunsmoor arrived in Minnesota around 1854. He was instrumental in the founding of the Harmony Mission (later Richfield Methodist Episcopal Church) in Richfield, where Lincoln settled. Dunsmoor's homestead included part of Minnehaha Creek, and so he would have been located near later Lincoln property.[33]

By November of 1860, George W. Lincoln was a ferryman with real estate valued at $200. He continued to board, now at the Thomas and Sarah Adams house. Adams was a farmer in Richfield Township, which is adjacent to Fort Snelling, with $500 worth of real estate and personal goods worth $250. Franklin Steele operated a ferry, and it is possible that he employed Lincoln.[34]

Around 1865, George Lincoln or Lincolin settled down and married Vinette, who was also born in Maine. By 1870 he was the father of Bertha, age four, and baby Florence, age one. Both girls were born in Minnesota. In the 1870 census, Lincoln listed his occupation as farmer; he still resided in Richfield Township.[35]

An 1866 map labels the G. Lincoln farmstead at Coldwater Spring. A later map, from 1870, appears to assign the initial "C". Based on other documents, it seems clear that it was the George W. Lincoln farmstead. (Figure 5.) Of particular note in this regard is Special Order 34 dated June 1867:

> Mr. George W. Lincoln now residing near the Cold Spring upon the military reservation of Fort Snelling is hereby permitted to cultivate for himself as agent of Franklin Steele Esq. a tract of ground situated about a mile west or southwest of said Lincoln's residence, and within the military reservation of Fort Snelling as established by survey of October 1853 said tract to contain not exceeding 150 acres. Mr. Lincoln is also permitted to enclose this tract with a fence which will be forfeited to the United States upon failure to remove it after five (5) days notice from the Commanding Officer of Fort Snelling to vacate the tract. This permit will not entitle the occupant of the ground to any claim whatever to the property nor to erect thereon any structure more than is herein authorized. This forgoing is subject to the approval of the Secretary of War.[36]

According to Vinette Lincoln's 1916 obituary, the family homestead included Minnehaha Falls and "extended along Minnehaha Creek from Lake Nakomis to the falls." The Andreas Atlas, published in 1874, shows Lincoln to be a property owner at Minnehaha Falls, and an 1879 map shows two George W. Lincoln parcels, one where Minnehaha Creek flows into the Mississippi River and a 38 acre parcel along the south shore of Rice Lake.[37]

As early as 1857, George Lincoln was in the area around the confluence of the Mississippi and Minnesota rivers. Through his work as a ferryman, he had the opportunity to know Franklin Steele. While it has not been determined precisely how Lincoln came to have a farmstead at Coldwater Spring, it is possible that he obtained the property from Steele.

CONFLICT NEAR & FAR

Wartime often calls for extraordinary measures, and the needs of wartime combined with the financial reverses of Franklin Steele brought Fort Snelling back under governmental control. In April, 1861, Governor Alexander Ramsey determined that Fort Snelling would be the rendezvous point for the First Minnesota. The fort was again a military installation, not a farm site or other private operation. During the Civil War, new soldiers were mustered in at the fort and received military training there before they received orders and shipped out. The fort continued to see military uses, including as a supply post, and the final contingent was mustered out late in 1866.[38] During the Civil War, Coldwater Spring remained an important source of drinking water for Fort Snelling.

Steele also continued to have use of an important ferry point during this period, and the non-federal uses of the general area persisted. Following the close of the Civil War, Steele and the federal government eventually (in 1871) settled on a division of the property. Steele received 6,400 acres and the federal government retained 1,520 acres, having concluded that the fort had military value after all. The Coldwater Spring was included in the Fort Snelling reservation.[39]

While the Civil War raged, Minnesota residents found themselves embroiled in more than one conflict. In addition to the rather distant campaigns against the Confederate states, the Dakota conflict occurred in 1862 within the state's borders. A series of violent clashes took place between the Dakota and the US military.[40]

Fort Snelling continued its role as a point of communication and assembly during the Dakota Conflict that dated from 1862. For example, after word of Dakota attacks reached the Twin Cities, Governor Ramsey rushed to confer with officers at Snelling. The various forts in the state played different roles in the short-lived conflict: Forts Snelling was "the rendezvous for raw troops," Ridgely, "the door the Sioux could not open," Ripley, the "wedge between Sioux and Chippewa," and Abercrombie saw little action but its presence to the west was a restraining influence. As a unit, the forts were seen as "basic to the frontier defense."[41]

In the aftermath of the brief but violent Dakota uprising, hundreds of Native Americans were imprisoned, and 38 were hanged at Mankato in December 1862. Meanwhile, many Dakota remained "huddled in camps near Fort Snelling." White Minnesotans feared the continued presence of the Dakota and worked to have them removed from the state. In February 1863 Congress simply put aside earlier treaties and expelled the Dakota from Minnesota.[42]

DEPARTMENT OF DAKOTA

To deal with military matters in the developing West, the federal government established the Department of Dakota in 1866. Briefly located at Fort Snelling, it was associated with efforts to modernize and expand the facilities but also the role of the fort regarding westward expansion in the postwar period. By 1881, the department was responsible for the Dakota and Montana territories as well as the state of Minnesota, overseeing troop movement, supplies distribution, and other administrative needs. The administrative offices of the Department of Dakota were variously located in St. Paul and Fort Snelling, returning to St. Paul in 1886. Regardless of the address, the Department of Dakota was an important administrative extension of Fort Snelling activities, including waterworks construction at the Coldwater Spring.

Around 1880, "extensive buildings" were constructed at the fort with the intention that the department would be permanently re-located there. According to a government report submitted December 4, 1879, an estimated $35,000 was appropriated for barracks and quarters the previous year.[43] The directive to move the Department of the Dakota to

Fort Snelling prompted the development of the "New Fort" outside the walls of the old garrison. Among the new buildings were Officers' Row, a headquarters building (1879), ordnance depot (1880), and new barracks (completed by 1885).[44]

The flurry of new construction reflected Fort Snelling's new role as host to the Department of the Dakota but also notable changes in the design and use of Army installations. For reasons that are unclear, the Department of the Dakota moved its administrative operations back to St. Paul in 1886.

WATERWORKS SYSTEM

Despite the departure of the Department of the Dakota offices, the period between 1880 and 1895 saw an important shift at Fort Snelling in the quality of daily life, including improved housing and treatment of the enlisted man. In the interests of efficiency and economy, some posts had closed and the total number across the country decreased dramatically. In 1881 there were 190 posts, around 1896, only 77. Those, such as Fort Snelling, that did make the cut received markedly improved housing and living conditions. At Fort Snelling, the expansion of the New Fort included development of a modern waterworks within the fort reserve.[45]

One factor in the decision to improve army posts across the country was the need to attract and retain qualified military personnel. Providing attractive barracks which had steam heat and plumbing and other creature comforts, such as those constructed at Fort Snelling, was one tactic in the campaign to improve the nation's military.[46]

A December 4, 1879, government report by Lieutenant S.R. Douglas offered insight into the development of the fort's water system at Coldwater Spring and underscored the vital importance of water to the fort.

> The water is obtained from a spring about three-quarters of a mile from the post, by means of water wagons. Water is also obtained from the Minnesota River, being forced through pipes by an engine, into a large tank on the west side of the parade ground, but the water thus obtained is unfit for drinking purposes.[47]

An earlier document, from January 19, 1866, described in great detail the difficulties inherent in obtaining drinking water from Coldwater Spring:

> A great improvement might be effected in the method of supplying the post with water from which it is now dependent upon a spring about 1600 yards from the fort. Water wagons are employed to supply the necessary wants of the garrison and public animals. Each wagon requires, to render it efficient, six horses and two men and the number of wagons thus each day continually employed has varied from four to ten, dependent upon the strength of the garrison. The road which these wagons necessarily travel

is a difficult one and upon the breaking up of winter requires much repairing to render it even passable. It is believed that it would cost less to introduce this water into the fort by lead pipes than to maintain four water wagons with their horses, etc. in good condition for one year. And the difference would become even more striking were account taken of the labor expended in repairing the road.

The spring being situated several feet above the level of the parade the scheme is rendered practicable. The desire to curtail the expenditures in all the branches of the government renders it desirable.[48]

As part of the major expansion of the fort, military officials acted on Hall's recommendations. During the early 1880s at Coldwater Spring, a modern pressurized water system, including a reservoir, part-stone water tank, and pump house, was constructed. The engineer's house shown on maps and photographs from the 1880s may have already been by the spring when the waterworks was constructed; if so, it likely was the George W. Lincoln farmhouse. Maps by E.B. Summers in 1882 and ca. 1879-89 show the fort's waterworks in place. There is a water tank, reservoir, a long narrow building for storage, and the house for the waterworks engineer. (Figure 6, Plates 1 and 3.)

The many improvements transformed Fort Snelling from a rather small scale supply depot to a modern, late 19th century military installation. The Camp Coldwater site underwent a similarly dramatic shift, from squatter camp and then farm site to modern waterworks. That the federal government was willing to invest in a modern waterworks, up-to-date housing, and other major construction marked a considerable shift in the evolution of Fort Snelling.

From the onset, it appears that the Coldwater waterworks was intended to offer an ancillary function as a recreational or leisure time destination. Historic photographs dated ca. 1885 show a small, attractive stone spring house located at a corner of the reservoir. The spring house is even shown on some maps from the period. It had a hipped roof, centered round arches with keystones, and was built of rough hewn large stone blocks. One of the photos appears to show a man in a small boat or skiff floating on the reservoir, and a woman and child look to the camera from benches in the pavilion.[49] (Plates 1 and 2.)

A detailed map from ca. 1895-98 shows important aspects of the waterworks and reveals that there has been more than one engineer's quarters. The map labels Building H3 the "burned Eng. Qrs.," and also depicts the "new eng's qrr," (number not yet assigned), circular water tank (H2), the reservoir, and the pump house building adjacent to the reservoir (H1). Even the small stone spring house is shown on this remarkably detailed rendering. A rail line with spur to the waterworks from the railroad that was located between it and the river is also present. Elsewhere on the map is the information that the pump house is wood, the water tank has a stone base with a wood tank above, and the engineer's quarters (H3) is constructed with wood. (Figure 7.)

The brick engineer's residence (H3) was constructed in 1899 to replace the burned wood house. The 802 square foot replacement building, which cost $2119.00, was more fireproof, having brick walls, and a stone foundation. There were 2/2 windows with segmental brick arches, possibly stone window sills, a central brick chimney, and a simple wood porch across the front. Gable-front in configuration, the house was located on a hill apparently above the reservoir area.[50] (Plate 4.)

Fort Snelling building records provide additional details about the waterworks. The 2,313 square foot pump house (H1) had a daily capacity of 921,600 gallons and cost $13,900 to construct around 1879-80. It had wood walls and a partial stone foundation, wood shingle roof, and wood floors. The pump house had large storage areas for coal and wood.[51] (Plate 3.)

It does not appear that the waterworks operations were extraordinary. Fueled by a coal-fired engine, the pumps drew water from the reservoir for storage in the water tower(s) whose height and placement resulted in sufficient water pressure to supply the fort below. The pump house was located west of the reservoir.

Around 1900, another wooden water tank, this one on tall steel supports, was added to the waterworks complex to provide additional water pressure. The new tank is shown in a ca. 1905 photograph (Plate 3) as well as a ca. 1900 photo that captured both old and new water tanks. A 1902 map adds the "new water tank" and shows the pump house with attached and labeled shed as well as the labeled reservoir located on lower ground than the tanks. A 1912 map shows much the same arrangement.[52] (Plate 4, Figure 8.)

Despite the addition of a second water tank, water needs at Fort Snelling exceeded the capacity of the Coldwater waterworks system. By 1904 the fort was also using water "pumped from an artesian well at the base of the bluff along the Minnesota River." This Minnesota River pumping station was used from around 1904 until 1930, at which time the fort began contracting for water from the City of St. Paul. A pump house at the Minnesota River edge is shown on a map dated December 20, 1904.[53]

The second water tank and the old pump house were razed in 1920 according to Fort Snelling building records. The waterworks were obsolete, for the fort purchased its water from the City of St. Paul. An eight inch water main on the Fort Snelling bridge provided the water. For emergency use, there was also a line connected to the City of Minneapolis by means of the nearby Veterans Hospital complex developed in the 1920s.[54]

Some of the structures and buildings of the Coldwater waterworks remained standing for some time. In the 1930s, the original water tank was converted to an ammunition storage facility; by 1937 the Army considered it to be in poor condition. Although its roof has long been gone, the reservoir spring house remains, as does the deteriorated reservoir. Renamed Building 252 in the 1930s, former Building H3, the brick engineer's quarters still stood in the 1950s when the Bureau of Mines began developing the area.[55]

To meet the medical needs of World War I veterans, the Veterans Bureau (later the Veterans Administration) obtained 165 acres of the Fort Snelling reservation in 1926. A large hospital complex with seven buildings arranged in a U-shape was dedicated on April 9, 1927. The 165 acres were north of Coldwater Spring and the waterworks system.[56] The hospital was another governmental use of the original reservation near Camp Coldwater.

COLDWATER PARK

Significant portions of the waterworks at Coldwater Spring were removed around 1920, and the area became open space. It was labeled Coldwater Park on 1927, 1935, and 1938 maps. (Figures 9 and 10.)

Historic photographs from the 1880s show area residents visiting Coldwater Spring as a leisure activity. Beginning in the first decade of the 20th century, Minneapolis residents could have taken the electric streetcar line to the park. The line is shown west of the park on maps from 1903 and 1905 and in a 1904 or 1905 photograph. The later map labels it the "electric line to Minnehaha & Minneapolis."[57]

The presence of a park melds well with the increasing recreational uses available at Fort Snelling. During the late 1930s and into the 1940s, military personnel and in some cases the general public enjoyed use of a polo field, nine-hole golf course, baseball stadium, and a large game preserve where hunting and fishing were possible.[58]

END OF FEDERAL FORT SNELLING ERA

On October 14, 1946, Fort Snelling was finally decommissioned and turned over to the Veterans Administration which used some of the buildings for medical care. In 1961 the VA turned over the fort to the State of Minnesota, and in 1965 restoration of portions of the fort began.

While the actual fort portion of Fort Snelling eventually became the responsibility of the State of Minnesota, Coldwater Spring became part of another federal agency, the Bureau of Mines. In 1957, Congress appropriated funds for a research center intended to foster the development of low-grade mineral resources such as taconite and peat. The initial portion of what became the Twin Cities Research Center opened in 1959. Historic Coldwater Spring is located on the grounds of the TCRC.

NATIVE AMERICANS AND CAMP COLDWATER

Introduction

The search for the earliest documentary evidence of Native American associations with Coldwater Spring has been elusive. Historic maps, contemporary accounts, and the work of other researchers and archeologists do not provide significant documented associations with the spring. Robert Clouse, who has researched Fort Snelling for decades, noted that "Although likely utilized by Native Americans for a very long period before Euroamericans arrived, no direct archaeological evidence for pre-contact use of the [Coldwater] spring is known."[59] Of course, the absence of evidence does not mean that Native Americans never used the area.

Descriptions of the Area

That the spring at Camp Coldwater was one of many in the immediate area may account for its general absence from Native American-related descriptions of the area. According to the explorer Zebulon Pike, "The shores [of the Mississippi above the Minnesota River] have many large and beautiful springs issuing forth, which form small cascades as they tumble over the cliffs into the Mississippi."[60]

Many visitors to the area around the Minnesota and Mississippi rivers described the various Native American sites they encountered, including the sacred or culturally significant sites between Fort Snelling and St. Anthony Falls. They do not, however, mention Camp Coldwater Spring. Typically, the falls of St. Anthony were mentioned along with the overall beauty of the scenery. Some also mentioned Minnehaha Creek and its falls as well as Morgan's Mound or Bluff. When Jonathan Carver visited the area in 1766, he and a Winnebago walked from the confluence of the Minnesota and Mississippi rivers to the Falls of St. Anthony because ice prevented using their canoe. The Native American had never visited the falls, but upon their arrival he immediately became most reverential. Carver did not mention Coldwater Spring although the pair would have passed near it.[61]

Writing to a friend early in 1835, Samuel Pond described the route from Fort Snelling to his home on the southeast side of Lake Calhoun. "Leaving fort Snelling and traveling northwest you would cross a green and level prairie three miles wide when you would come to a beautiful stream of water....called by the Indians "the little river." Pond fails to mention Coldwater Spring or any Native American presence, and the map he drew in 1834 also excluded any reference to the Camp Coldwater area.[62]

Mary Eastman, wife of the Fort Snelling's commanding officer Seth Eastman, recorded the following, also making no mention of Coldwater Spring:

The Indians call them Mine-hah-hah, or "laughing waters." In sight of
Fort Snelling is a beautiful hill called Morgan's Bluff; the Indians call it
"God's House." They have a tradition that it is the residence of their god
of waters, whom they call "Unk-ta-he." [The hill] commands on every
side a magnificent view.[63]

Writing from the same period when Eastman was at the fort, the 1840s, Harriet
Bishop described the St. Louis House at Coldwater Spring in some detail and also
mentioned that "Morgan's Bluff, one mile to the right [of the post cemetery] is a
sacred spot."[64] Bishop made no mention of Native American names or uses of
Coldwater Spring.

Encampments & Visits

Several commentators mentioned a Native American presence in the Fort Snelling
environs. It appears that the location of the fort, approximately 40 miles south of the
boundary line for Dakota and Ojibwe lands was selected to be convenient to both groups.
(The site was also the reasonable limit for steamboats.) "The role assigned to U.S.
government representatives by both Ojibwe and Dakota as intermediary between them
meant the fort and its surroundings served as a kind of neutral or middle ground, in the
literal sense a geographical space in which it was possible to mediate politically."[65]

In their detailed study of the Fort Snelling environs in 1838, White and White noted that
Nicollet's 1837 map of the area seemed to show Native American encampments at the
trading houses of Baker and Sibley. Baker's trading house, of course, was at Coldwater
Spring; these encampment sites seem to be related to the presence of a trader, not a
sacred spot. White and White also noted that artwork in general typically depicted
encampments (if they are represented at all) at Sibley's trading house in Mendota or
below the fort.[66]

Benjamin F. Baker traded with both the Dakota and Ojibwe, but it appears that the
Ojibwe were more likely to camp at his place by Coldwater Spring. We know that
August 2, 1838, Patrick [Peter?] Quinn and his Ojibwe wife had a house near the large
stone Baker trading house, and six fellow Ojibwe visited when they came to the fort.[67]

Especially in lean times, the Dakota came to the fort and camped in large villages
awaiting annuity payments or other assistance. Perhaps because they were familiar with
the area, Native Americans living around Lac qui Parle, came to spend the winter "on the
site of old Camp Coldwater, knowing that only from the fort could they obtain relief
[from harsh winter conditions]."[68]

In a book published in 1835, Charles Joseph Latrobe stated that "lodges of the Sioux and
the Chippewas encamped near the Reservation, or near the trading houses." These would
have been temporary visits, if only because the Dakota and the Chippewa were enemies

unlikely to reside near one another except for brief visits to traders, the Indian Agency, or the fort.[69]

The falls of St. Anthony, then a splendid sight, was known to both the Dakota and the Ojibwe, and both groups had given it descriptive names. Oanktehi, the god of waters and evil, was said to reside in this sacred place but could also emerge from springs.[70]

Summary

In 1855, Chief Seattle of the Duwamish tribe, stated that "Every shiny pine needle, every sandy shore, every mist in the dark woods, every clearing and humming insect is holy in memory and experience of my people."[71] While every tribe is different, strong associations with natural resources are a constant theme. Within that context, Coldwater Spring, like all other natural manifestations, may have been viewed as spiritually important to some Native Americans. We find no evidence that the area and the spring have had specific Native American names nor have they been tied to specific spirits or spiritual practices historically.

Based on documentary evidence, Camp Coldwater was the place where some Indians camped temporarily when they visited the Baker trading house, Fort Snelling, and the Indian Agency. These visits would have occurred primarily in the 1820s-1840s. As more and more land was ceded to the federal government and Native Americans were forced out of Minnesota, there was a decreasing need to come to the fort to conduct business.

By the 1850s, the area around Coldwater Spring was being settled on and owned by Euro-Americans. During the time when Baker's post was in operation, however, Native Americans likely obtained water from the nearby spring. Native Americans are among the several groups who have occupied or visited the Coldwater Spring vicinity.

[1] Theodore Blegen, *Minnesota. A History of the State*, 2nd ed. Minneapolis: University of Minnesota Press, 1975, p. 99; William Watts Folwell, *A History of Minnesota*, 4 vols. (St. Paul: Minnesota Historical Society, 1921; reprint ed., St. Paul: Minnesota Historical Society, 1956), 1:137; Donald Dean Parker, ed. *The Recollections of Philander Prescott*. Lincoln: University of Nebraska Press, 1966, p. 30.

[2] Folwell, 1:140; Blegen, *Minnesota: A History*, p. 100; George E. Warner and Charles M. Foote, *History of Hennepin County* (Minneapolis: North Star Publishing Company, 1881), p. 163; Charlotte O. Van Cleve. *"Three Score Years and Ten," Life-long Memories of Fort Snelling Minnesota...* (Minneapolis: Harrison & Smith, 1888), p. 32.

[3] Blegen, *Minnesota: A History*, pp. 92-3; Folwell, 1:216.

[4] Blegen, *Minnesota: A History*, pp. 92-3; Folwell, 1:216.

[5] Folwell, vol. 1, p. 216, quoting Baker to Taliaferro, July 16, 1823, Taliaferro Papers.

[6] Folwell, vol. 1, p. 217.

[7] Folwell, 1:161-2.

[8] Robert Clouse, *Archaeological Research at the Former Twin Cities Bureau of Mines Testing Facility, Minnesota*. Prepared for the National Park Service. Draft report, August 2001, p. 41; Works Progress Administration, *The WPA Guide to Minnesota* (St. Paul: Minnesota Historical Society Press, reprint ed. 1985), p. 137.

[9] Donald Dean Parker, ed. *The Recollections of Philander Prescott*. Lincoln: University of Nebraska Press, 1966, p. 168.

[10] White and White, pp. 155-160.

[11] Folwell, 1:218, quoting Lt. E.K. Smith to Plympton, October 19, 1837, in *Sale of Fort Snelling Reservation*, Appendix 13.

[12] The August 16, 1837 memorial or petition is reproduced, without attribution, in Clouse, *Archeological Research....*, 2001, pp. 42-43, and can be found in *Sale of Fort Snelling Reservation*, 14 (serial 1372), according to Follwell, 1:217. Additional research can be found in White and White, *passim*; and *Minnesota Beginnings. Records of St. Croix County, Wisconsin Territory, 1840-1849* (Stillwater, Minnesota: Washington County Historical Society, 1999), *passim*.

[13] Folwell, 1:218, 220-1.

[14] Folwell, 1:223. Folwell directs the reader to *Wiskonsan Territory—Settlers on the Military Reservation near Fort Snelling* (27 Congress, 2 session, *House Reports*, no. 853 – a) serial 410.

[15] Lucy L.W. Morris, ed. *Old Rail Fence Corners. Frontier Tales Told by Minnesota Pioneers* (N.p.: Minnesota Society of the Daughters of the American Revolution; reprint ed., St. Paul: Minnesota Historical Society, 1976), pp. 9-10; *Minnesota Beginnings*, p. 327.

[16] Folwell, 1:196-7; *Old Rail Fence*, p. 22.

[17] Theodore Blegen, "The 'Fashionable Tour' on the Upper Mississippi," *Minnesota History* 20 (1939): 377-396.

[18] Mrs. Elizabeth Ellet, *Summer Rambles in the West* (New York: J.C. Ricker, 1853), p. 393.

[19] Harriet Bishop, *A Floral Home; or, First Years of Minnesota* (New York: Sheldon, Blackman & Company, 1857), p. 160.

[20] Fuller, George F. Plan of the Military Reserve at Fort Snelling Under the Direction of James W. Abert. Undated but thought to be ca. 1853. MHS MSS C22, Folder 1.

[21] Harriet Razada Godfrey, "St. Louis House." 1930. MHS MSS FF612.H58S6.G58.

[22] Godfrey.

[23] Harriet Razada Godfrey, "St. Louis House," 1930." Includes January 31, 1930 letter from Moffett to Godfrey.

[24] Folwell, 1:503.

[25] Folwell, 1:503-5.

[26] Folwell, 1:504-507.

[27] Excerpt from 1868 report to U.S. House of Representatives in Clouse, *Archeological Research*, 2001, p. 48.

[28] White and White, pp. 157-160.

[29] Fowler, 1:513, 433.

[30] Fowler, 1:434; Moncure, Thomas. Map of the City of Fort Snelling, Minnesota, at the Confluence of the Mississippi and Minnesota Rivers. Surveyed August 1857.

[31] Morris, p. 170.

[32] Census of Minnesota, Hennepin County, 1857; Kennebec County, Maine court records (online).

[33] Mary Gram, "History of Richfield Methodist Church," *Hennepin County History* 5 (January 1945):6.

[34] U.S. Census, Hennepin County, 1860.

[35] U.S. Census, Hennepin County, 1870; Minnesota State Census, 1865.

[36] U.S. Army Commands, Special Orders Nos. 33 and 34, Department of Dakota, June 1867. From National Archives Record Group 98. MHS MSS P333, Box 5.

[37] Mrs. Lincoln Rites Tuesday," Minneapolis *Journal*, December 31, 1916, p. 8; A.T. Andreas, *Illustrated Historical Atlas of the State of Minnesota* (Chicago: A.T. Andreas, 1874), p. 42; George F. Warner and George W. Cooley. *Map of Hennepin County, Minnesota.* Minneapolis: Warner & Foote, 1879.

[38] Fowler, 1:433; Blegen, *Minnesota. A History*, pp. 240-242.

[39] Fowler, 1:433-4.

[40] Blegen, *Minnesota. A History.* pp. 259-284.

[41] Blegen, *Minnesota. A History*, pp. 275, 270.

[42] Blegen, p. 280.

[43] Warner and Foote, pp. 162, 165.

[44] Clouse, *Archeological Research*, p. 29.

[45] Clouse, *Archeological Research*, pp. 29, 31.

[46] Jack D. Foner, *The United States Soldier Between Two Wars: Army Life and Reform, 1865-1898* (New York: Humanities Press, 1970), pp. 77-95.

[47] Warner and Foote, p. 165.

[48] Brvt. Maj. Robert H. Hall to Lt. David Scott, ADC Headquarters District of Minnesota, St. Paul, January 19, 1866.

[49] Coldwater Spring photographs, MH5.9.F1.3CW.r3; MH5.9.EN3CW.r2; MH5.9.F1.3CW.r6, MHS.

[50] United States, Army, Quartermaster Corps, Fort Snelling Building Records, ca. 1905-ca. 1969, in MHS MSS, alphabetical section of the manuscripts. Fort Snelling records dated June 30, 1940 included a photograph of the house, showing that the original porch had been replaced with an enclosed version and there was a rear one story enclosed portion trailing to the rear.

[51] United States, Army, Quartermaster Corps, Fort Snelling Building Records, ca. 1905-ca. 1969, in MHS MSS, alphabetical section of the manuscripts. The dimensions for the pump house were as follows: main building, 41' x 26', storage portion, 21'3" x 84'4", boiler room, 25' x 25', coal shed, 12' x 72', wood shed 12' x 12'. It is unclear from the form whether the boiler room was part of the main building, and how the coal and wood sheds related to the storage area.

[52] Clouse, *Archeological Research*, p. 50.

[53] Clouse, *Archeological Research*, p. 54.

[54] United States, Army, Quartermaster Corps, Fort Snelling Building Records, ca. 1905-ca. 1969, in MHS MSS.

[55] Clouse, *Archeological Research*, pp. 33, 50; United States Army, Quartermaster Corps, Fort Snelling Building Records, ca. 1905-ca. 1969, in MHS MSS.

[56] 50th Anniversary, Veterans Administration Hospital, Minneapolis, Minnesota, 1927-1977. Pamphlet.

[57] MHS photograph HE4.2 M1.

[58] Dale F. Becker, "Fort Snelling, 1938-1945," B.A. paper, University of Minnesota, 1983, pp. 3-10.

[59] Clouse, *Archeological Research*, p. 39.

[60] Robert Clouse, "Fort Snelling, Minnesota: Intrasite Variability at a 19th Century Military Post" (Ph.D. dissertation, University of Illinois, 1996), p. 126, quoting explorer Zebulon Pike.

[61] Edward Neill, *Dakotah Land and Dakotah Life* (Philadelphia: J.B. Lippincott & Company, 1858), p. 208.

[62] Samuel W. Pond to Herman Hine, January 19, 1835. MHS.

[63] Mary Eastman, *Dahcotah or, Life and Legends of the Sioux around Fort Snelling.* New York: John Wiley, 1849; reprint ed. Afton: Afton Historical Society, 1995, p. 2.

[64] Harriet Bishop. *A Floral Home; or, First Years of Minnesota.* New York: Sheldon, Blakeman & Company, 1857, p. 160.

[65] White and White, p. 117.

[66] White and White, pp. 127, 43.

[67] Folwell, 1:151, 152-3; Marcus Hansen, *Old Fort Snelling* (Minneapolis: Ross and Haines, 1958), p. 125.

[68] Hansen, pp. 109-110.

[69] Charles Joseph Latrobe, *The Rambler in North America*, 2 vols.. (New York: Harper & Brothers, 1835) 2:215.

[70] Lucille Kane. *The Falls of St. Anthony....* St. Paul: Minnesota Historical Society Press, 1987. p. 2; Edward Neill, *Dakotah Land and Dakotah Life* (Philadelphia: J.B. Lippincott & Company, 1858), p. 56.

[71] Michael Dougherty, *To Steal a Kingdom. Probing Hawaiian History* (Waimanalo, Hawaii: Island Style Press, 1992), p. 97.

3. FINDINGS & RECOMMENDATIONS

INTRODUCTION

The focus of this study has been on the land around Coldwater Spring. We wanted to know who used the property, including in relation to developments associated with Fort Snelling, and how and when they were present. Regardless of the theme, which might fall outside the NHL and NRHP nominations, we included it in the Coldwater Spring study. For example, no mention is made in the NHL and NRHP nominations about George Lincoln and his farmstead, but it is surely part of the Coldwater Spring story. The NHL nomination for Fort Snelling addresses one theme in detail, the military use of the area from 1819-1858 and 1861-1946, as does this historical study. The NHL nomination also mentions briefly nonmilitary settlers, fur traders, tourists, as does this historical study in some detail. The NHL nomination mentions famous people who have served at or visited Fort Snelling and also discusses Dred Scott, who was later to figure in matters leading up to the Civil War; this historical study does not make mention of famous people associated with Fort Snelling unless they were associated with Coldwater Spring.

Both the NHL nomination and the NRHP nomination were prepared prior to the development of standards and guidelines now in place for the preparation of NHL and NRHP nominations. They do not therefore address or justify or define historical developments using current guidelines outlined in the National Register Bulletin, How to Complete the National Register Registration Form. As noted, the NHL context is military. The NRHP nomination checks multiple areas of significance and, more or less, discusses them in the text. They are Historic Aboriginal, Commerce, Communications, Military, Political, Transportation, and Other (Settlement of Frontier). We have tried to discuss these topics in this report, but only as they relate to the Coldwater Spring locale. Our focus was on address the topics and format specifically outlined in the Scope of Work for the Project.

We have attempted to frame statements of significance in the broad themes mentioned in the NHL and NRHP nominations, but with subcontexts that, we hope, serve to further develop the historic contexts. For example, under the Military Context, we have identified four subcontexts: Camp Coldwater, Daily Life at a Military Installation, Changing Perceptions of Appropriate Federal Military Policy, and Military Reforms—as they relate to the Coldwater Spring environs.

SIGNIFICANCE OF THE COLDWATER SPRING SITE

The Coldwater Spring vicinity is a site that contributes to the significance of the Fort Snelling NRHP Historic District, the Fort Snelling National Historic Landmark, and the Old Fort Snelling (state) Historic District. It is significant as the location of important historic activities directly associated with Fort Snelling for more than a century. These historic activities are diverse and include military, commercial, settlement, and recreational historic functions. Not only are the activities varied, they date from the earliest permanent presence of the U.S. military in the area, 1819, and continue until the close of direct military responsibility for the site, 1946. The Coldwater Spring site, which includes a reservoir ruin, contributes to our understanding of the broad patterns of American history as they relate to the arrival of the U.S. government in present Minnesota and the impact of that presence on many levels.

The Coldwater Spring site enhances the previously listed NHL and NRHP historic character and should be regarded as a contributing element in both the NHL and NRHP nominations. Despite a number of changes to the landscape and the removal and addition of a number of buildings, the site retains integrity of location, design (the reservoir and spring house), setting, materials (spring house), feeling, and association. The Coldwater Spring site was the location of significant events and prehistoric and historic activities. As a site, it possesses historic, cultural, and archeological value regardless of the value of any existing structure.

While demonstrably important to our understanding of the multiple layers of Fort Snelling and environs history, the site does not appear to be individually eligible for listing in the NRHP (or as an NHL). The Coldwater Spring site draws its significance from its associations with the fort, as an important component of the compelling story of the many layers of history of the fort and vicinity.

PERIODS OF USE

The various historic functions of the Coldwater Spring site and the general periods of time involved are discussed in this section. Key phases are identified with asterisks. The Scope of Work stated that land uses should be categorized in terms of public and private use and they are therefore so identified below.

Government Use
    Military
        Camp Coldwater, 1820-ca. 1823**
        Daily Life at a Military Installation, 1820-1920**
        Changing Perceptions of Appropriate Federal Military Policy, 1861-71
        Military Reforms, 1880-1920**
    Entertainment/Recreation
        Coldwater Park, 18801-1946

Non-Government Use
    Exploration/Settlement
        Settlers, 1821-1840**
    Commerce
        Baker Trading Post, ca. 1833-1841**

St. Louis Hotel, ca. 1841-1862**
Lincoln Farmstead, ca. 1857-ca. 1871

Periods of Government Use, by Historic Function

Military

Camp Coldwater, 1820-ca. 1823**

Albeit a brief period of occupation, the establishment of Camp Coldwater at the spring allowed the construction of the original portion of Fort Snelling. The military selected the site by a spring to be the base of operations during construction activities. As such, it is strongly associated with the circumstances behind construction of Fort Snelling.

Daily Life at a Military Installation, 1820-1920**

Coldwater Spring was more than the locus of an early military encampment; it provided drinking water to Fort Snelling personnel for one hundred years. For decades, soldiers drew water from the spring and hauled it in wagons down to the fort. After around 1880, the Coldwater Spring waterworks was constructed, of which the reservoir ruin and associated stone spring house are the most prominent remnants. The waterworks were apparently razed in 1920 when the fort began obtaining water from the City of St. Paul. The role of Coldwater Spring in providing water to the fort over an extended period of time illustrates patterns of daily life at the fort and changes in how the water was supplied to Fort Snelling.

Changing Perceptions of Appropriate Federal Military Policy, 1861-1871

Between 1857 and 1861, the federal government had vacated the Fort Snelling Military Reserve. The decision to sell the reserve was based on perceptions that the fort was no longer of value to the government. With the onset of the Civil War, those perceptions rapidly changed, and the government resumed control.

This period is also associated with the actual military role of Fort Snelling during the Civil War and the Dakota conflict. It continues the story of the various activities and events that took place during an important period of American and Minnesota history. The Coldwater Spring site does not appear to have had a significant role in these events.

Military Reforms, 1880-1920**

Alarmed at the growing rate of desertions among enlisted men, the U.S. military took steps to retain soldiers. A fundamental part of these steps was improving daily life on military posts. These improvements included construction of better quality barracks, the provision of adequate plumbing and heating, and imposing more sensible rules of conduct. The construction of the Coldwater Spring waterworks in 1880 was a direct response to these military reforms that took place at Fort Snelling and other forts in the late 19th century. The waterworks provided potable water to the fort until 1920. The US Army was transformed from a small frontier force to a major modern army.

Entertainment/Recreation

Coldwater Park, 1880s-1946

When the Coldwater Spring waterworks, with its attractive reservoir and attached stone spring house, were completed in the early 1880s, the place soon became a destination for leisure activities. It is possible that area residents had come to the springs to draw water prior to the changes, and the improvements to the spring simply encouraged further use of the area. After the waterworks was no longer used by the fort, the area was designated Coldwater Park, as shown on maps from the 1920s and 1930s. It is not clear if area residents continued to visit Coldwater Park after the fort's closure in 1946, but that year marks the end of military responsibility for the resource. That the Coldwater Spring waterworks performed double duty, as a water source for the fort and as a leisure-time destination for area residents, is an example of government and non-government use of the area. Although not a highly developed park, the area nonetheless provided a respite from daily life.

Periods of Non-Government Use

Exploration/Settlement

Settlers, 1821-1840**

Aware that Fort Snelling had been established at the juncture of the Mississippi and Minnesota rivers, settlers from the failed Selkirk colony moved down to the fort site beginning in 1821. Some stayed in the area briefly, while others took up residence illegally on land not yet available for settlement. Some settlers may also have had associations with fur traders who were clustered about the fort. Others worked for the Indian Agency as blacksmiths and interpreters or for Fort Snelling. One woman was highly esteemed for her midwifery abilities. A number of these settlers chose to live around Coldwater Spring. An 1837 census and map of the area showed some 82 residents at Camp Coldwater (including Massey's landing). The military removed all settlers as of 1840; others had been moving away as early as 1837 when the first census and map were completed.

The fort was a magnet for settlement. The presence of illegal settlers, sellers of liquor, and workers for the Indian Agency, fur traders, and the fort is an integral part of the early development of the Fort Snelling environs. Those who settled at Camp Coldwater illustrate how frontier settlement occurs, the recognized importance of a military installation during early settlement, and the variety of settlers present at an earlier, pivotal period in the history of the Fort Snelling environs.

Commerce

Fur Trading Activities, ca. 1833-1841**

The most prominent example was the Baker trading post, although other log buildings were also associated with the fur trade at Coldwater Spring. Benjamin F. Baker was an independent trader, that is, he was not a representative of one of the major fur trading organizations. He was involved in a variety of frontier-era pursuits, including logging, fur trading, and sutlering for the post. As early as 1833, he received licenses to trade with the Native Americans and he was living in the Coldwater Spring area then. Around 1837 he constructed a large stone trading house at Camp Coldwater, evidently in competition with H.H. Sibley's fine stone house. Independent fur traders are a fundamental part of the early history of Fort Snelling, Minnesota territory, and the commercial interests of early arrivals intent on tapping the natural resources of the area.

St. Louis Hotel, ca. 1853-1862**

After Baker died in 1839, his stone trading house evolved into the St. Louis Hotel. Newcomers to the Fort Snelling area were directed to the building for accommodation. As the region increasingly became a tourist destination during the steamboat era, the hotel was enlarged and continued to provide lodging. Mill workers also boarded at the St. Louis Hotel until it was destroyed by fire in 1862. The St. Louis Hotel is associated with important themes associated with the Fort Snelling area, including the well-publicized descriptions of scenic attractions, the commercial importance of the steamboat period of transportation, and the daily lives of mill workers in antebellum Minnesota.

Lincoln Farmstead, ca.1857-ca. 1871

The story of the Lincoln Farmstead is a curious one. It involves the 1857 purchase of the Snelling reserve by Franklin Steele, the time when the government simply assumed control of the reserve (1861-66), and the years when legal title to the reserve was in question, which was a period of lawsuits and negotiation between Steele and the federal government (1866-1871). By 1866, George W. Lincoln lived near Coldwater Spring on the military reservation. In 1867, he received permission to cultivate 150 acres on the reserve, as an agent of Franklin Steele. It has not been determined how long this arrangement persisted nor how long Lincoln lived in the farmhouse. It is possible that once negotiations between Steel and the government were concluded in 1871 that Lincoln was evicted. The first engineer's quarters of the Coldwater Spring waterworks may have been the former Lincoln farmstead. The Lincoln farmstead and the circumstances behind its use stand as an additional aspect of the many layers of land use, negotiations, changing federal policies, and occurrences that collectively constitute the development of the Fort Snelling area.

INTEGRITY MATTERS

Despite a number of changes to the landscape and the removal and addition of a number of buildings, the site retains integrity of location, design (the reservoir and spring house), setting, materials (spring house), feeling, and association. The Coldwater Spring site was the location of significant events and prehistoric and historic activities. As a site, it possesses historic, cultural, and archeological value regardless of the value of any existing structure. The location of the site, the area around a free flowing spring, is fundamental to its uses as an important water source for the fort and for nonmilitary settlers alike. The physical environment of the Coldwater Spring site reflects the very qualities that made the place desirable over time. In the early years, soldiers, illegal settlers, traders, Native Americans, and assorted travelers drew water from the spring. Later, its location overlooking Fort Snelling afforded the means for development of a waterworks, which was part of the military's efforts to provide improved living conditions on military installations. Some of the topographic features, vegetation, and relationship with the fort remain, as does the free flowing spring. The presence of Coldwater Spring, the reservoir, and the distinctive (though altered) stone spring house convey the property's historic character and evoke a feeling of the historic sense the property expresses. The associations that the Coldwater Spring site has with the historical development of Fort Snelling form a direct and important link to the past.

ARCHEOLOGICAL REMNANTS

Considerable changes in topography and land use have occurred in the Coldwater Spring vicinity, including construction of at least 15 buildings that are part of the TCRC campus. In addition, rail lines (now removed) have crossed the area. According to Robert Clouse, "significant portions of the property contain buried, intact, undisturbed topsoils" and some of these buried soils have 19th century artifacts. Four surface features have been identified, the reservoir, its spring house, the grading of a military rail spur to the waterworks, and a possible foundation remnant from the pump house.[1] Clouse conducted documentary research and a thorough archeological survey which addressed the purposes of the project, the findings of which were applied to this study.

Despite the cutting and filling that took place, it is possible that the remnants of six types of resources could be present on the Coldwater Spring site. There are a number of maps of the area, but they are of varying quality and detail. A combination of research—especially using maps—with archeological investigations might yield additional artifacts or remnants of the six property types listed below.

-- Camp Coldwater summer camp (said to be tents)
-- Households shown on 1837 Smith map, including outbuildings such as blacksmith shops and stables
-- Benjamin F. Baker trading post (later the St. Louis Hotel)
-- George W. Lincoln Farmstead
-- Railroad remnants

RECOMMENDED BOUNDARY CHANGE

As has been discussed in some detail, both here and elsewhere, the historic significance of the Coldwater Springs environs is recognized through a variety of mechanisms, some of them overlapping, some of them providing several types of significance for the same area. For example, the recommended boundaries for the proposed U.S. Bureau of Mines Twin Cities Research Center Historic District would overlap with the Fort Snelling-related districts. (See Figure 15.) Figures 11-13 show the boundaries for the Fort Snelling National Historic Landmark (NHL), Fort Snelling National Register Historic District (NRHP), and the Old Fort Snelling (State) Historic District. Documentation and maps regarding these boundaries are confusing and, at times, contradictory.

Figure 14 depicts proposed changes to the existing boundaries. The boundary changes encompass an area where historic events directly associated with Fort Snelling took place. In relation to NHL and NRHP boundaries, the change "bumps out" the existing boundaries just south of TCRC Building #1, a large cross-shaped building visible on USGS maps, and runs along north boundary of the TCRC, essentially along the roadway shown on USGS current maps. Certain lines in the proposed boundary change simply follow topographic contours, some of which are due to relatively recent landscaping. These are arbitrary lines of convenience and do not reflect any known historical use of occupation of the area in question. The changes are consistent with those recommended by Clouse as a result of his archeological study.

The expanded boundary brings in the entire Coldwater Spring site, including the reservoir ruin. This area has been the focus of a variety of important events and uses that contribute to the significance of the NRHP and NHL historic districts. By extending the boundary line west to the west property line, the area where a number of artifacts from the first half of the 19th century have been recovered is brought into the district(s).

The boundary change is delineated by a polygon whose vertices are marked by the following UTM reference points: A: 15 0484 490E, 4971 462N, B: 15 0484 498E, 4971 700N, C: 15 0484 529E, 4971 501N, D: 15 0484 448E, 4971 478N.

Existing district boundaries intrude into the TCRC property from the east. The recommended boundary changes extend in a north-south line that runs between the TCRC Building #1 and the Buildings #3 and #12 cluster which is south of Building #1. The boundary change runs along the west boundary of the TCRC property and continues to the south property line. There the boundary line turns south and continues to a point just east of Building #7 where it joins with existing NRHP and NHL boundaries. (Figure 14.)

---

[1] Clouse, *Archeological Research*, pp. 64-5, quoting p.65.

BIBLIOGRAPHY

Note: MHS refers to the Minnesota Historical Society.

Atwater, Isaac and John H. Stevens. *History of Minneapolis and Hennepin County*, 2 vols. New York: Munsell Publishing Company, 1895.

Becker, Dale F. "Fort Snelling, 1938-1945." B.A. paper, University of Minnesota, 1983.

Bishop, Harriet. *A Floral Home; or, First Years of Minnesota*. New York: Sheldon, Blakeman & Company, 1857.

Blegen, Theodore C. "The 'Fashionable Tour' on the Upper Mississippi." *Minnesota History* 20 (1939): 377-396.

Blegen, Theodore C. *Minnesota. A History of the State*, 2nd ed. Minneapolis: University of Minnesota Press, 1975.

Clouse, Robert. *Archaeological Research at the Former Twin Cities Bureau of Mines Testing Facility, Minnesota*. Prepared for the National Park Service. Draft report, August 2001.

------. "Fort Snelling, Minnesota: Intrasite Variability at a 19th Century Military Post." Ph.D. dissertation, University of Illinois, 1996.

Clouse, Robert and E.K. Steiner. *All That Remains: A Study of Historic Structures at Fort Snelling, Minnesota*. Prepared for Minnesota Department of Natural Resources. Draft report, 1998.

Coldwater Spring photographs. MH5.9.F1.3CW.r3; MH5.9.EN3CW.r2; MH5.9.F1.3CW.r6; HE4.2 M1, MHS.

Dougherty, Michael. *To Steal a Kingdom. Probing Hawaiian History*. Waimanalo, Hawaii: Island Style Press, 1992.

Eastman, Mary. *Dahcotah or, Life and Legends of the Sioux around Fort Snelling*. New York: John Wiley, 1849; reprint ed. Afton: Afton Historical Society, 1995.

Ellet, Mrs. Elizabeth. *Summer Rambles in the West*. New York: J.C. Ricker, 1853.

50th Anniversary, Veterans Administration Hospital, Minneapolis, Minnesota, 1927-1977. Pamphlet.

Folwell, William Watts. *A History of Minnesota*, 4 vols. St. Paul: Minnesota Historical Society, 1921; reprint ed., St. Paul: Minnesota Historical Society, 1956.

Foner, Jack D. *The United States Soldier between Two Wars: Army Life and Reform, 1865-1898*. New York: Humanities Press, 1970.

Godfrey, Harriet Razada. "St. Louis House." 1930. MHS MSS FF612.H58S6.G58.

Gram, Mary. "History of Richfield Methodist Church." *Hennepin County History* 5 (January 1945): 6.

Hansen, Marcus. *Old Fort Snelling, 1819-1858*. Minneapolis: Ross & Haines, 1958.

Hotopp, John A., *et al*. *A Cultural Resource Assessment of the Proposed Reroute for Trunk Highway 55 54th Street to County, Road 62, Hennepin County, Minnesota*. Report prepared for the Federal Highway Administration and MnDOT. 1999.

Kane, Lucille. *The Falls of St. Anthony....* St. Paul: Minnesota Historical Society Press, 1987.

Kennebec County, Maine court records (online).

Johnson, General Richard W. "Fort Snelling from its Foundation to the Present Time. *MHS Collections* 8 (1898): 427-448.

Latrobe, Charles Joseph. *The Rambler in North America*, 2 vols. New York: Harper & Brothers, 1835.

"Mrs. Lincoln Rites Tuesday." Minneapolis *Journal*. December 31, 1916.

Minnesota Beginnings. Records of St. Croix County, Wisconsin Territory, 1840-1849. Stillwater, Minnesota: Washington County Historical Society, 1999.

Census of Minnesota, Hennepin County. 1857.

Morris, Lucy L.W., ed. *Old Rail Fence Corners. Frontier Tales Told by Minnesota Pioneers*. N.p.: Minnesota Society of the Daughters of the American Revolution; reprint ed., St. Paul: Minnesota Historical Society, 1976.

Neill, Edward D. *Dakotah Land and Dakotah Life*. Philadelphia: J.B. Lippincott & Company, 1858.

Neill, Edward D. and J. Fletcher Williams. *History of the Upper Mississippi Valley*. Minneapolis: Minnesota Historical Company, 1881.

Ollendorf, Amy. *Twin Cities Research Center, U.S. Bureau of Mines*. Final Report. 1996. On file, MN SHPO, HE-96-09.

Parker, Donald Dean, ed. *The Recollections of Philander Prescott.* Lincoln: University of Nebraska Press, 1966.

United States Army. Special Order 33. MSS P333, Box 5. From NARG 98, U.S. Army Commands, Special Orders Nos. 33 and 34, Department of Dakota, June 1867.

United States Army. Quartermaster Corps. Fort Snelling Building Records, ca. 1905-ca. 1969, in MHS MSS, alphabetical section of the manuscripts.

United States Bureau of the Census. 1860, 1870.

United States Department of the Interior. *National Register Bulletin 16. Guidelines for Completing National Register of Historic Places Forms.* 1986.

Van Cleve, Charlotte O. *"Three Score Years and Ten," Life-long Memories of Fort Snelling Minnesota....* Minneapolis: Harrison & Smith, 1888.

Warner, George E. and Charles M. Foote. *History of Hennepin County.* Minneapolis: North Star Publishing Company, 1881.

White, Helen and Bruce White. *Fort Snelling in 1838: An Ethnographic and Historical Study.* Report prepared for Minnesota Historical Society. 1998.

Works Progress Administration. *The WPA Guide to Minnesota.* St. Paul: Minnesota Historical Society Press, reprint ed. 1985.

MAPS

(In chronological order). Most of the Fort Snelling maps are in MHS manuscript C22.

1821. Part of the Michigan and Missouri Territories at the Confluence of the Mississippi and St. Peters River, 1821. 1821. MHS MSS C22, Folder 6.

1823? A Topographical View of the Site of Fort Anthony at the Confluence of the Mississippi and St. Peters Rivers. [1823?]. Later notation: from Sibley papers. MHS MSS C22, Folder 7.

1835. Taliaferro, Lawrence. Map of the Fort Snelling Area. 1835.

1837. Smith, E.K. Fort Snelling and Vicinity, October 1837. MHS MSS C22, Folder 7.

1838. Smith, E.K. Map of a Proposed Reservation at Fort Snelling by E.K. Smith, U.S.A. March 25, 1838. MHS MSS C22, folder 1.

1839. Colby, R. Ames. Topographical View of a Portion of the Military Reserve, Embracing Fort Snelling. Ca. October and November 1839. MHS MSS C22, Folder 7.

1839. Topographical Survey of the Military Reservation Embracing Fort Snelling. Done October and November 1839 by Order of Major Plympton. MHS MSS C22, Folder 7.

1839. Map of the Military Reserve Embracing Fort Snelling. Done October and November 1839 by Order of Major Plympton. MHS MSS C22, Folder 1.

1839. Thompson, James L. Map of the Fort Snelling Military Reservation as Surveyed by Lieut. James L. Thompson in October and November, 1839 by Order of Major Plympton.

Ca. 1853. Fuller, George F. Plan of the Military Reserve at Fort Snelling Under the Direction of James W. Abert. Undated but thought to be ca. 1853. MHS MSS C22, Folder 1.

1856. Johnson, F? W. Military Reserve. Fort Snelling. May 27, 1856.

1857. Moncure, Thomas. Map of the City of Fort Snelling, Minnesota, at the Confluence of the Mississippi and Minnesota Rivers. Surveyed August 1857. MHS G4144.F6751857.M652.

1857. Seth Eastman. Map of the Military Reservation of Fort Snelling, Minnesota.

1866. Military Reserve, Fort Snelling.

1874. Andreas, A.T. *Illustrated Historical Atlas of the State of Minnesota*. Chicago: A.T. Andreas, 1874.

1879. George F. Warner and George W. Cooley. *Map of Hennepin County, Minnesota*. Minneapolis: Warner & Foote, 1879. MHS G4143.H4G461879.W2.

1879-89. Summers, E.B. Fort Snelling. 1879-89.

1880. Military Reservation of Fort Snelling, Minnesota. 1880. MHS MSS C22, Folder 9.

1882. Summers, E.B. Map of Fort Snelling Reservation. 1882. MHS MSS C22, Folder 9.

1885-93. Map of Fort Snelling Reservation, 1885-93. On map: "print of an old map, furnished by HQ77th Corps Area, Omaha, Nebraska, November 1937." The 1893 date had clearly been added at some point to the original map.

Ca. 1895-98. Fort Snelling Reservation. Partial copy in SHPO files.

1902. Fort Snelling Reservation. MHS C22.

1903. Topographic Map of the Military Reservation Fort Snelling, Minnesota. 1903. MHS MSS C22, Folder 5.

1904. Fort Snelling, Minnesota, December 20, 1904. MHS MSS C22, Folder 9.

1905. Fort Snelling Military Reserve. Partial copy in SHPO office.

1912. Revised Map of Fort Snelling, Minnesota, January 9, 1912. 1912. MHS MSS C22.

1927. W.H. Honnold, *et al.* 1927 Map of Fort Snelling and Vicinity. National Archives Record Group 77, Sheet 43-Minn. Copy made from Hotopp report.

1934. Nyland, J.G. and A.J. Wattzelt. Fort Snelling Environs. Copy made from Hotopp report.

1938. Fort Snelling and Environs. 1938. Blueprint. MHS MSS P2394, Box 3.

Fort Snelling, Minnesota Buildings and Utilities. 1938. MHS MSS C22.

FIGURES & PLATES

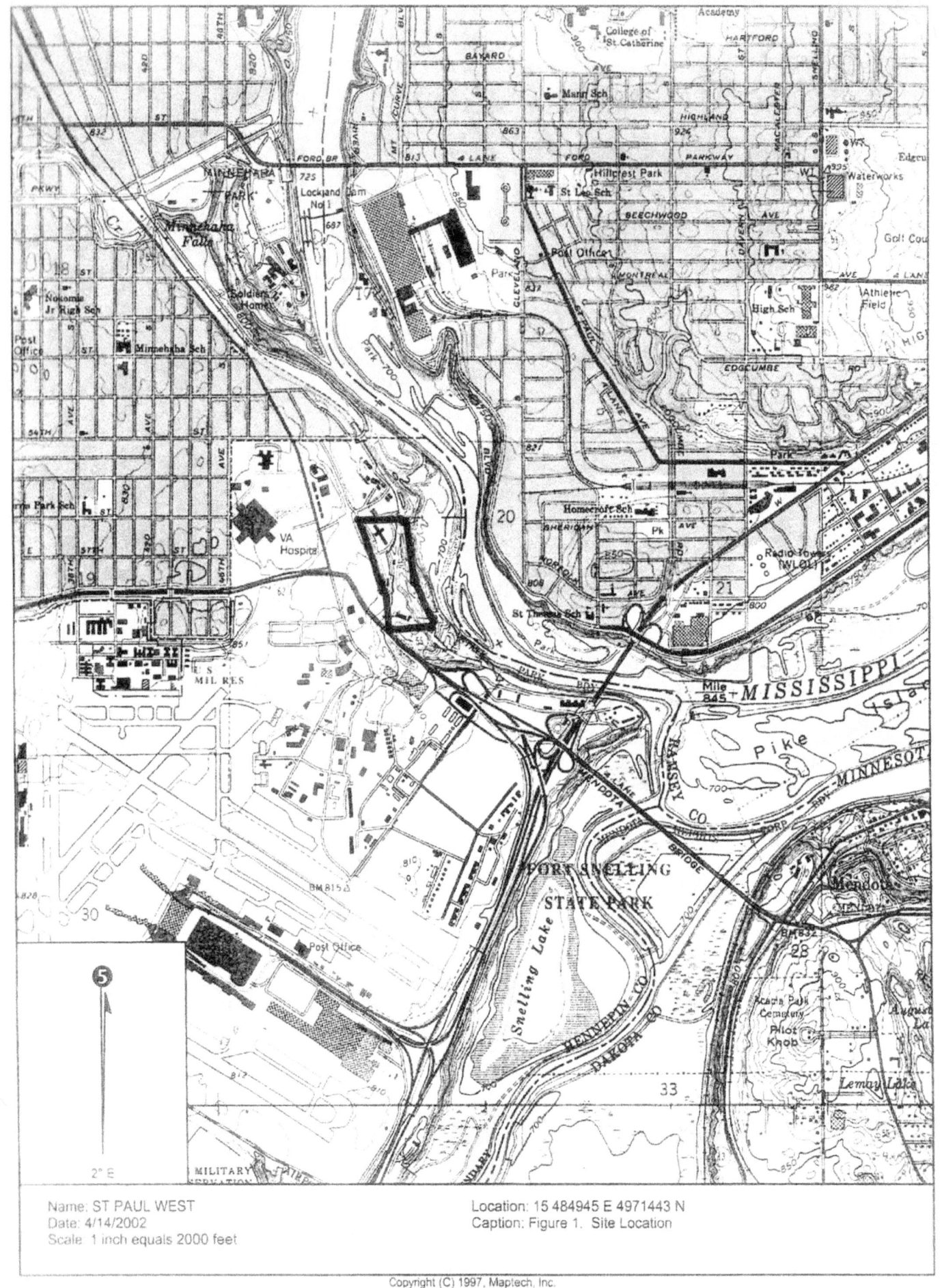

Name: ST PAUL WEST
Date: 4/14/2002
Scale: 1 inch equals 2000 feet

Location: 15 484945 E 4971443 N
Caption: Figure 1. Site Location

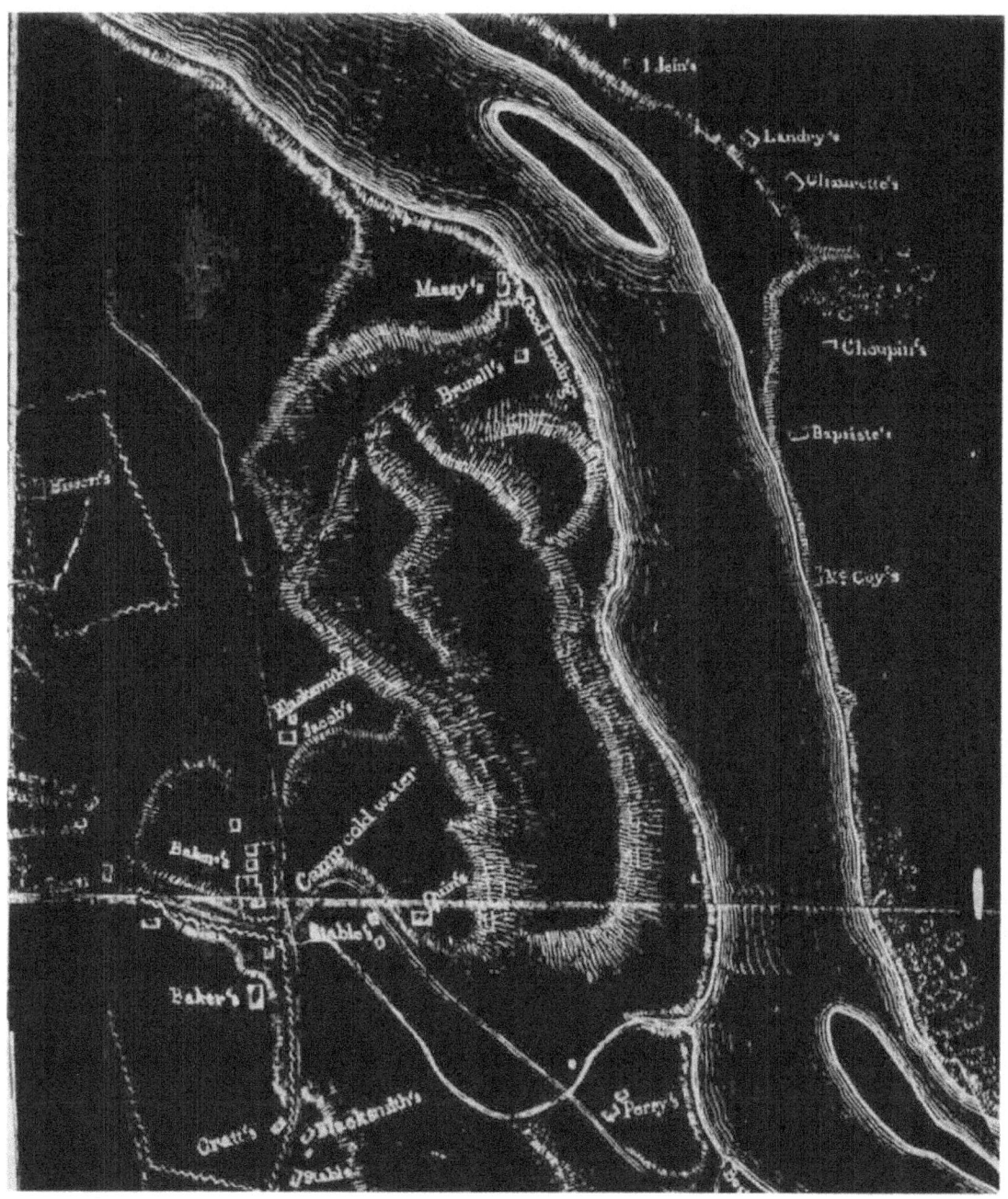

Figure 2. E.K. Smith. Fort Snelling and Vicinity, October 1837. The only known map showing locations of specific named properties at Camp Coldwater. The rendering reveals the extent of the Camp Coldwater settlement prior to the eviction of settlers.

Figure 2

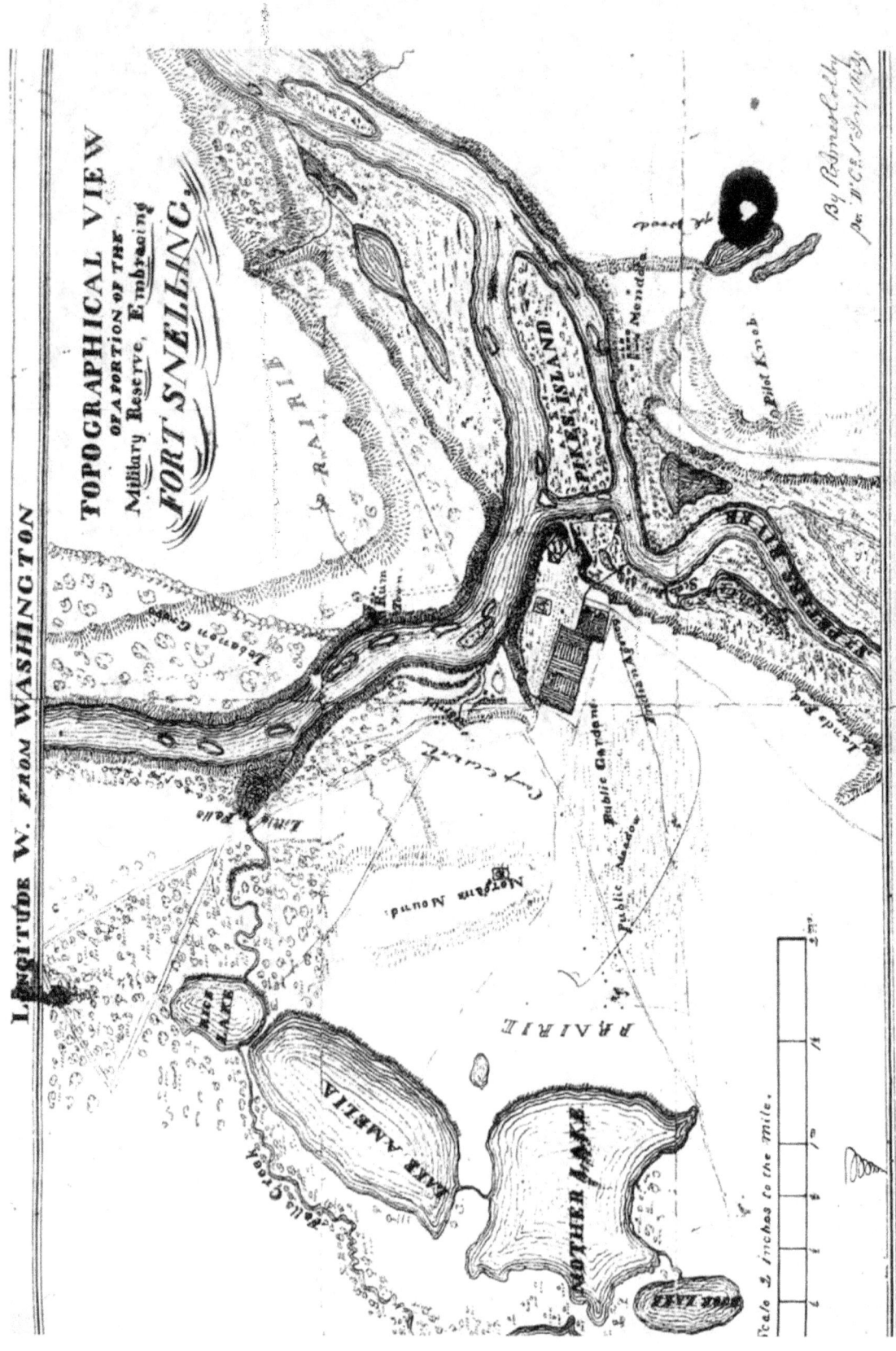

Figure 3. R. Ames Colby. Topographical View of a Portion of the Military Reserve, Embracing Fort Snelling. Ca. October and November 1839. Map provides overall setting of Camp Coldwater area, including Morgan's Mound, Rum Town on the east bank, the Indian Agency, fort, and Mendota trading house. The scattered buildings at Camp Coldwater are not identified.

Figure 4. Fuller, George F. Plan of the Military Reserve at Fort Snelling under the Direction of James W. Abert. Ca. 1853. "Hotel", the former Baker trading post, is shown by Coldspring. Portion of larger map.

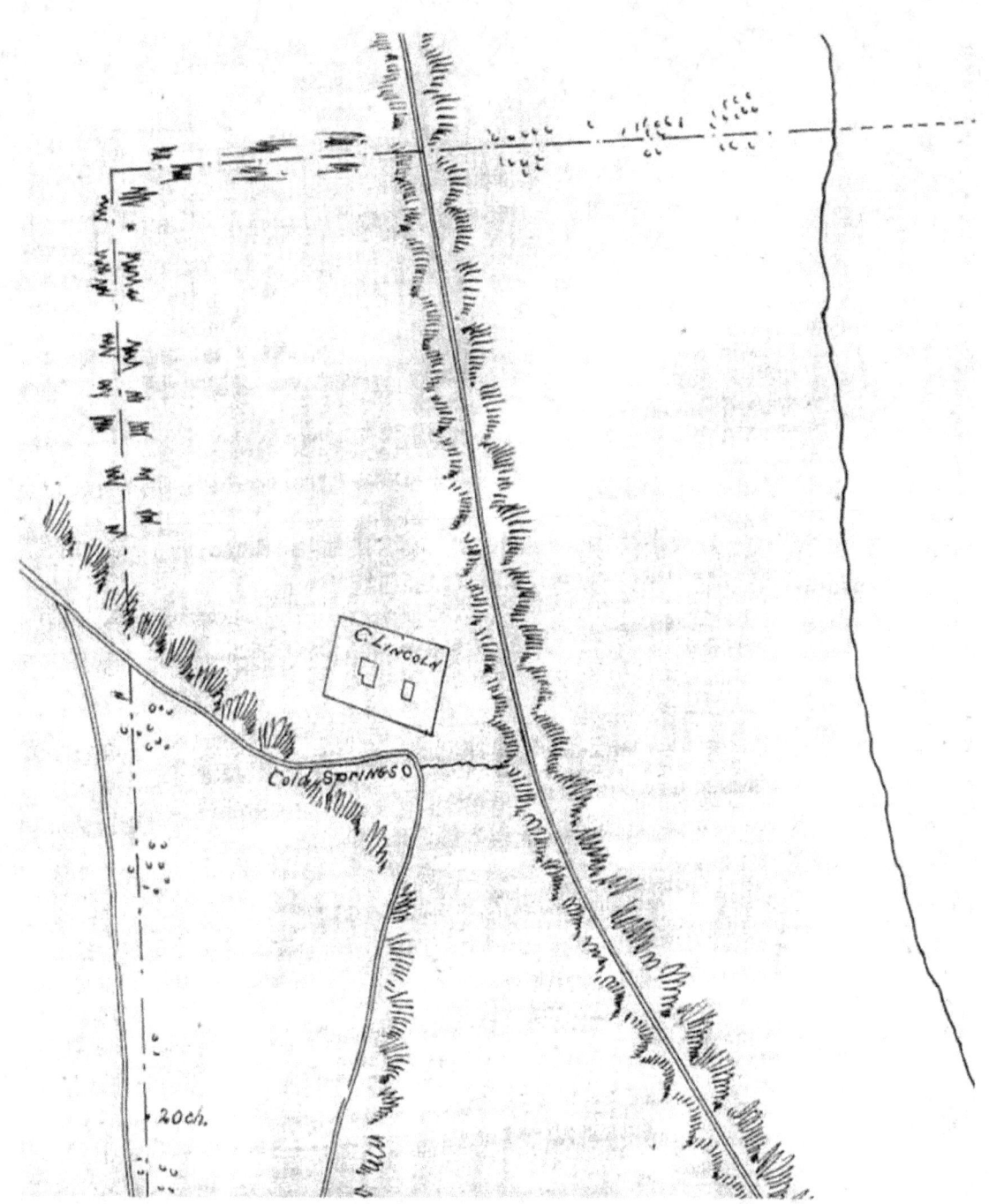

Figure 5. Map of the Military Reserve of Fort Snelling, Minnesota. Ca. 1870. Copy made from Mn SHPO files. Shows farmstead of "C. [G.] Lincoln" located at the Cold Springs. Portion of a larger map.

Figure 5

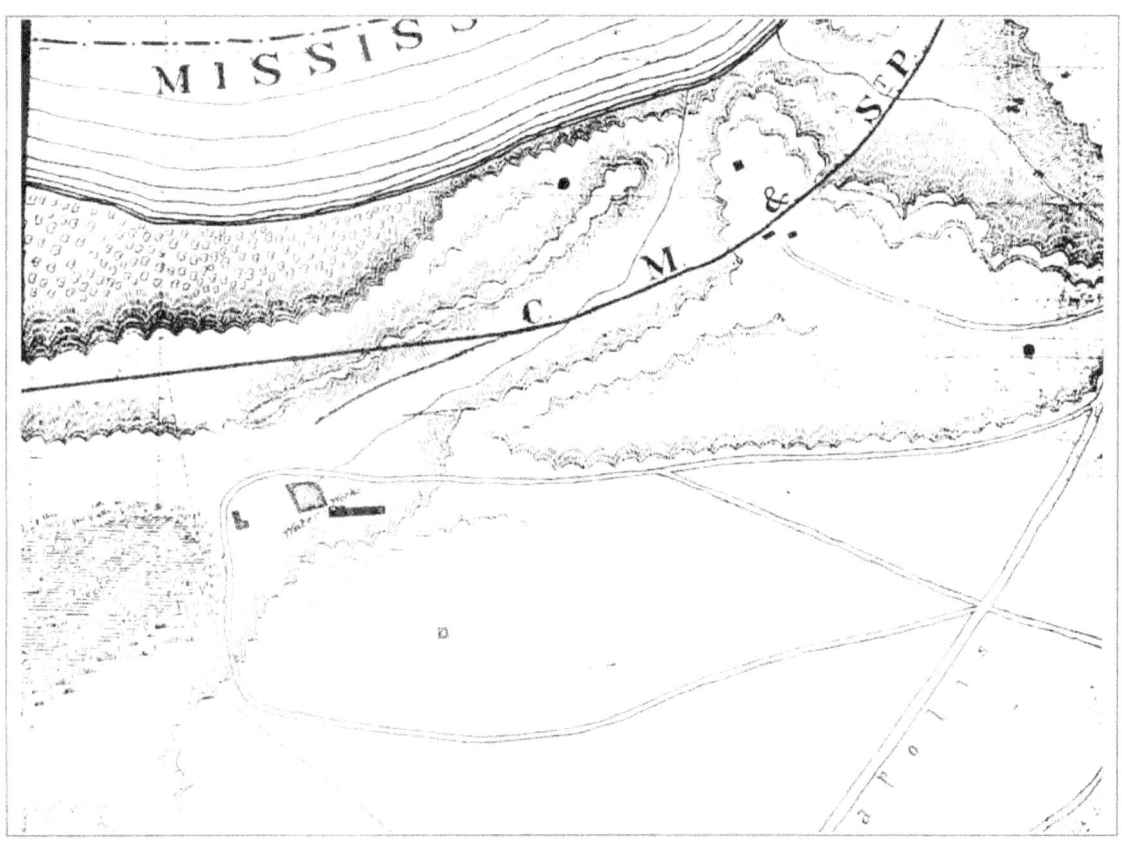

Figure 6. E.B. Summers. Map of Fort Snelling Reservation. 1882. Waterworks reservoir and pump house in place, also stone water tank above the waterworks. Probable former Lincoln farmhouse shown. Portion of larger map.

Figure 6

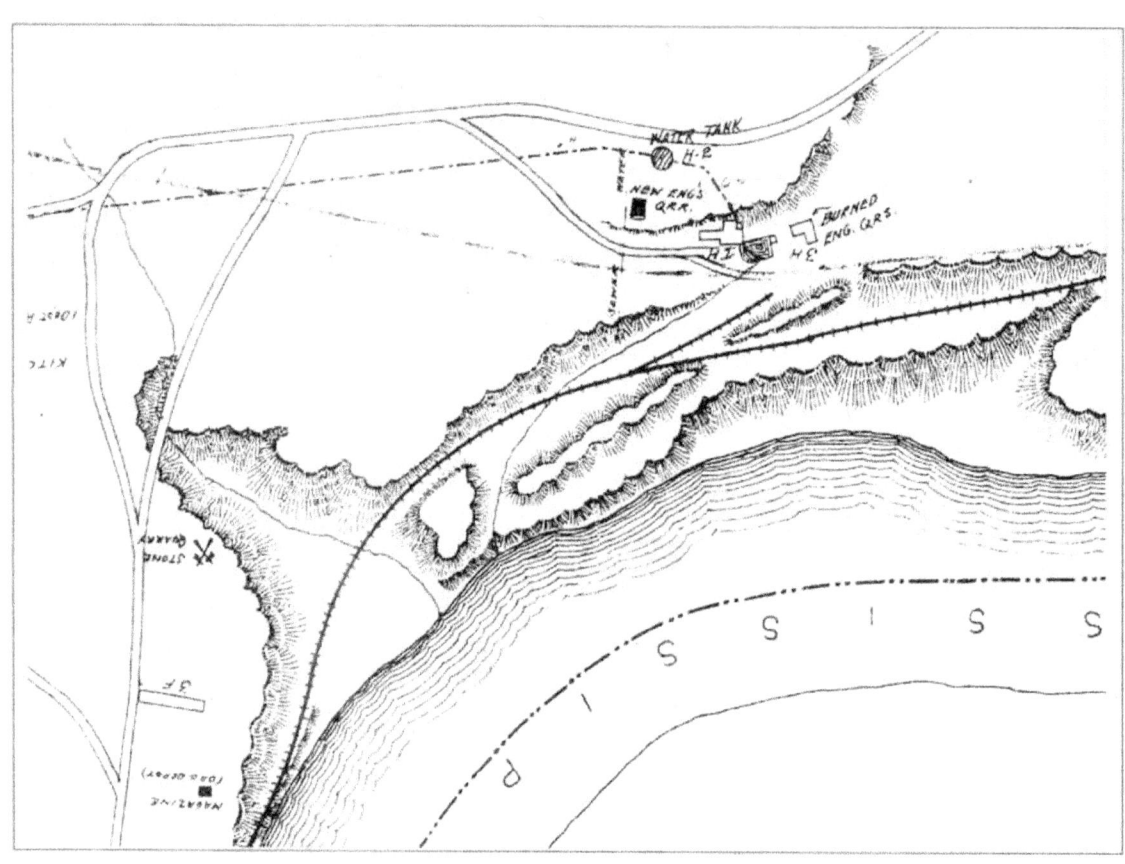

Figure 7. For Snelling Reservation. Ca. 1895-98, Copy from SHPO files. Burned and replacement engineer's quarters shown at the waterworks. Buildings and structures labeled H1, H2, and H3. Portion of larger map.

Figure 7

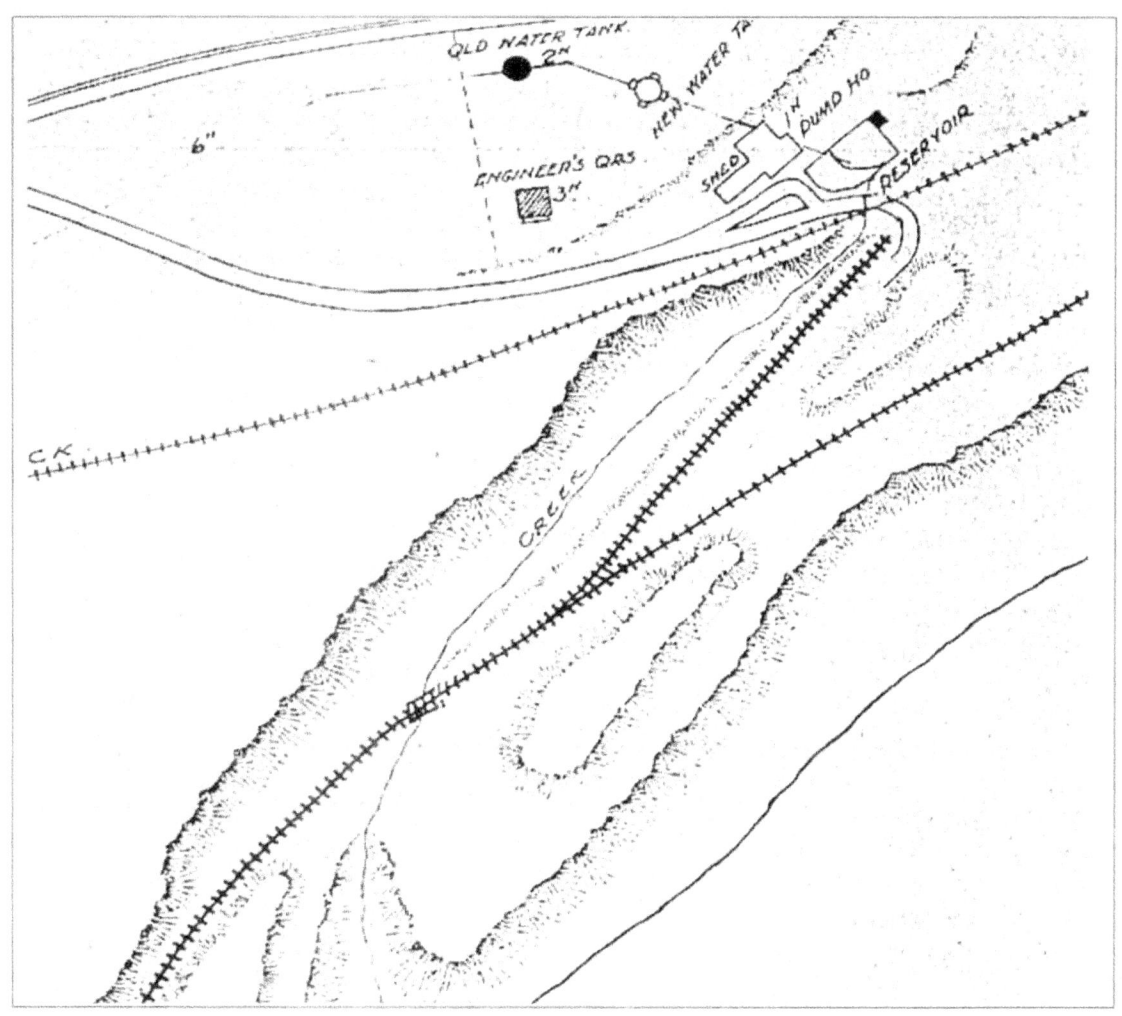

Figure 8. For Snelling Reservation. 1902. Copy from SHPO files. Second water tank in place. Portion of larger map.

Figure 8

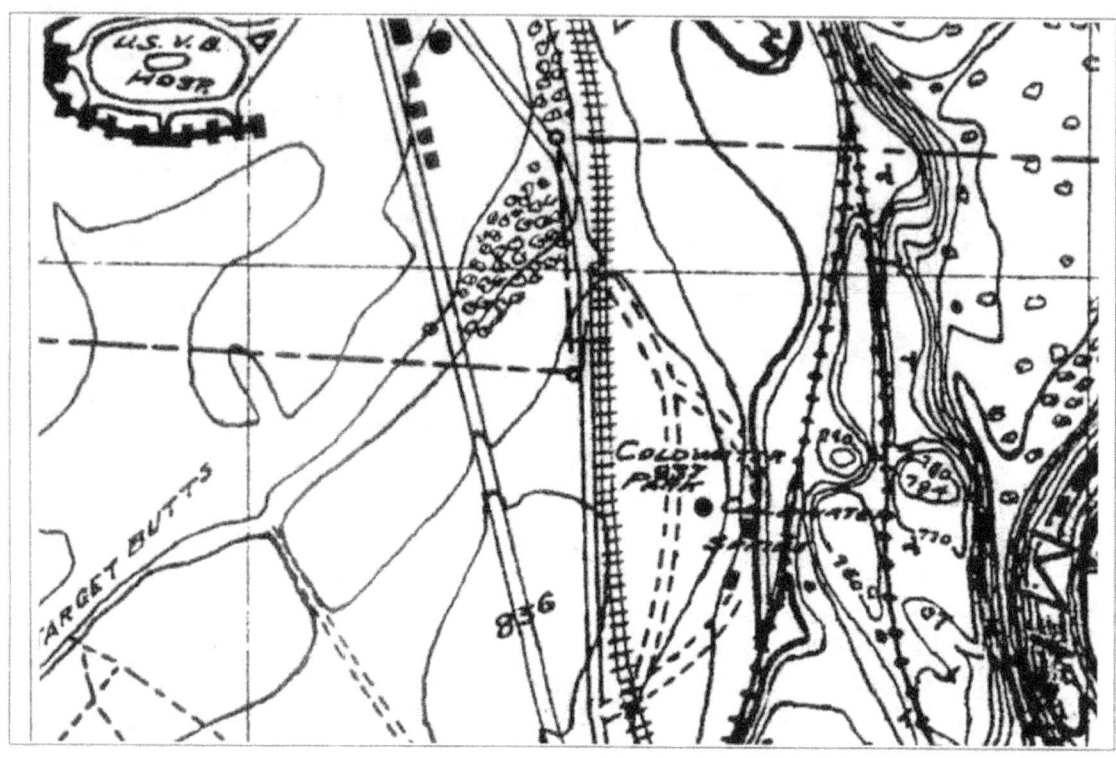

Figure 9. W.H. Honnold, *et al.* Map of Fort Snelling and Vicinity. 1927. Copy made from Hotopp report. Conversion of property to Coldwater Park with Coldwater Spring shown. Trolley line is located to west of the park. Portion of larger map.

Figure 9

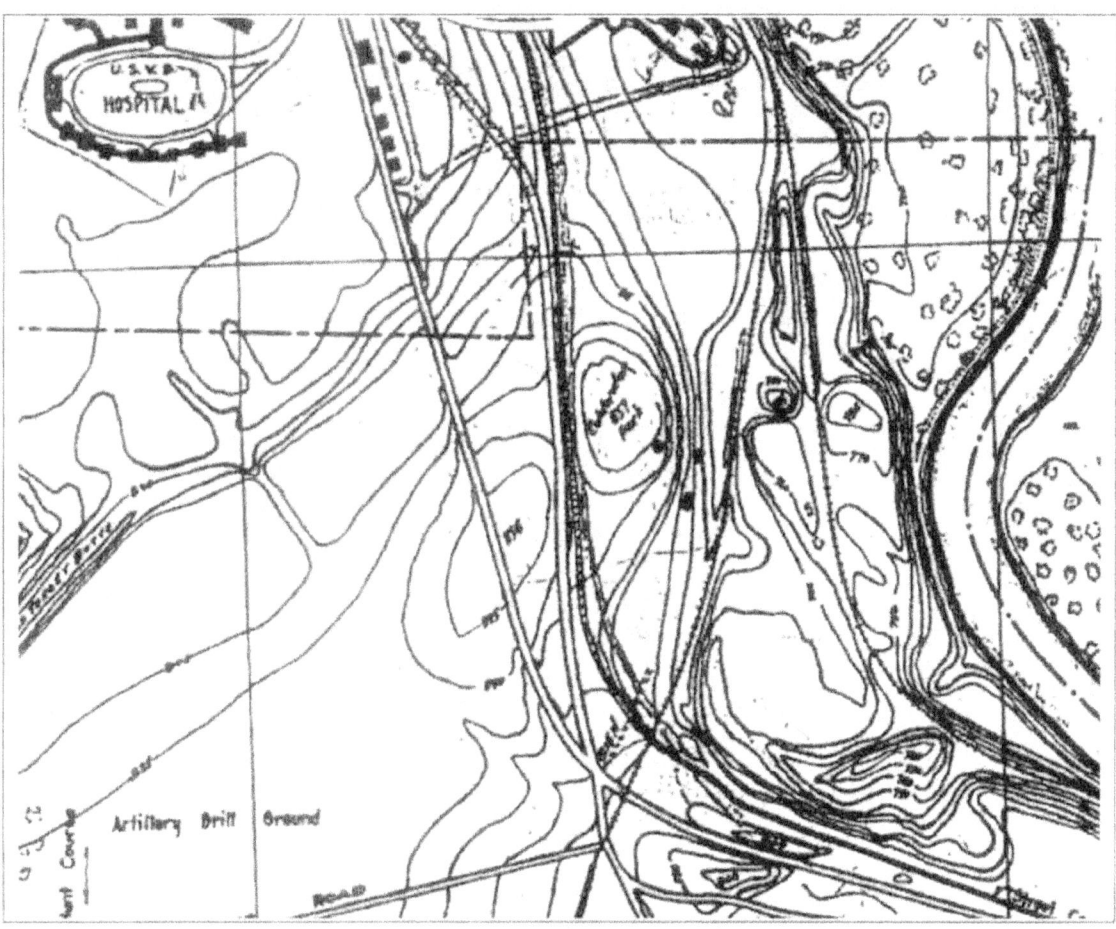

Figure 10. Nyland, J.G. and A.J. Wattzelt. Fort Snelling Environs. 1934. Copy made from Hotopp report. Coldwater Park shown southeast of Veterans Hospital. Portion of larger map.

Figure 10

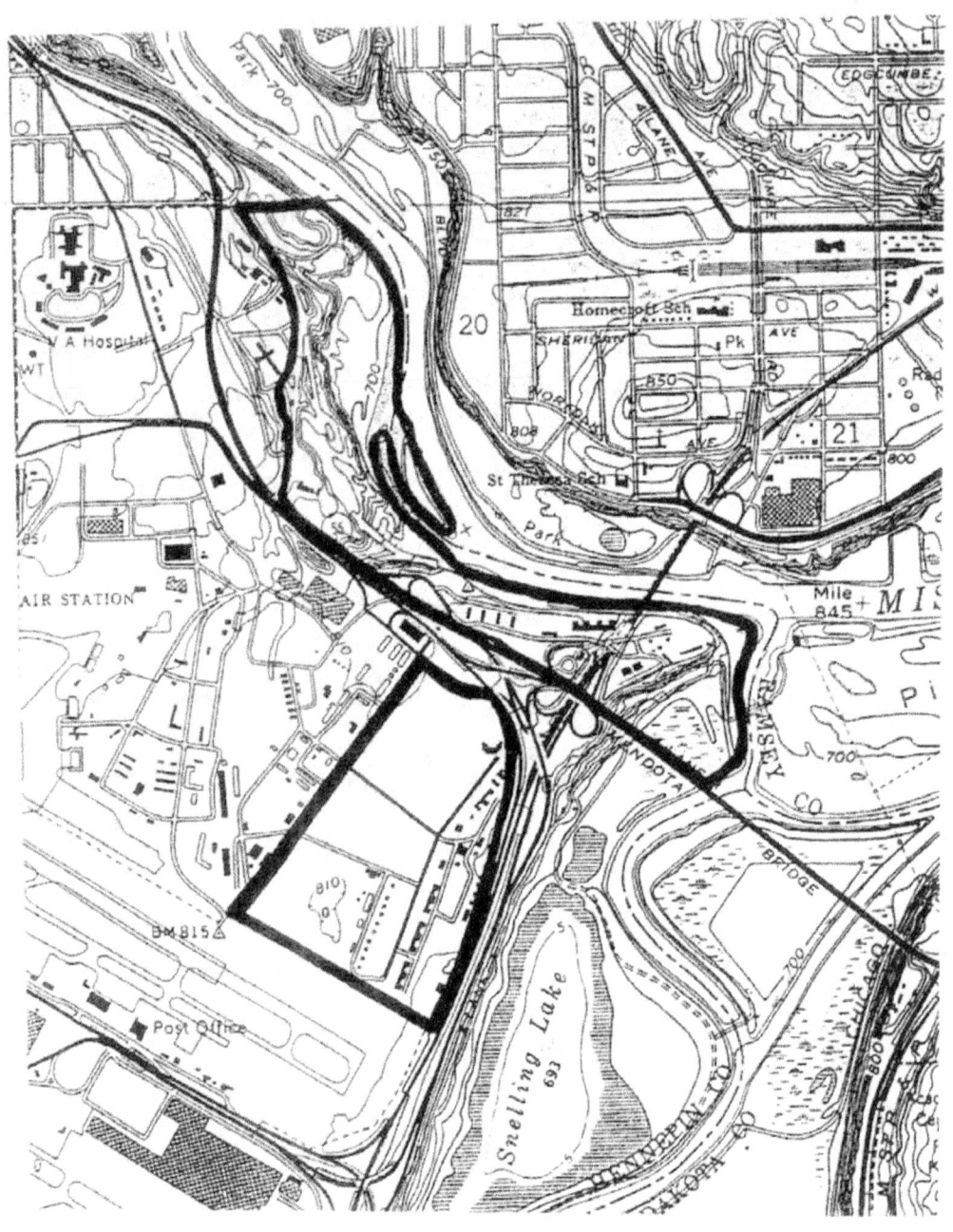

Figure 11. Fort Snelling National Historic Landmark Boundaries

Figure 11

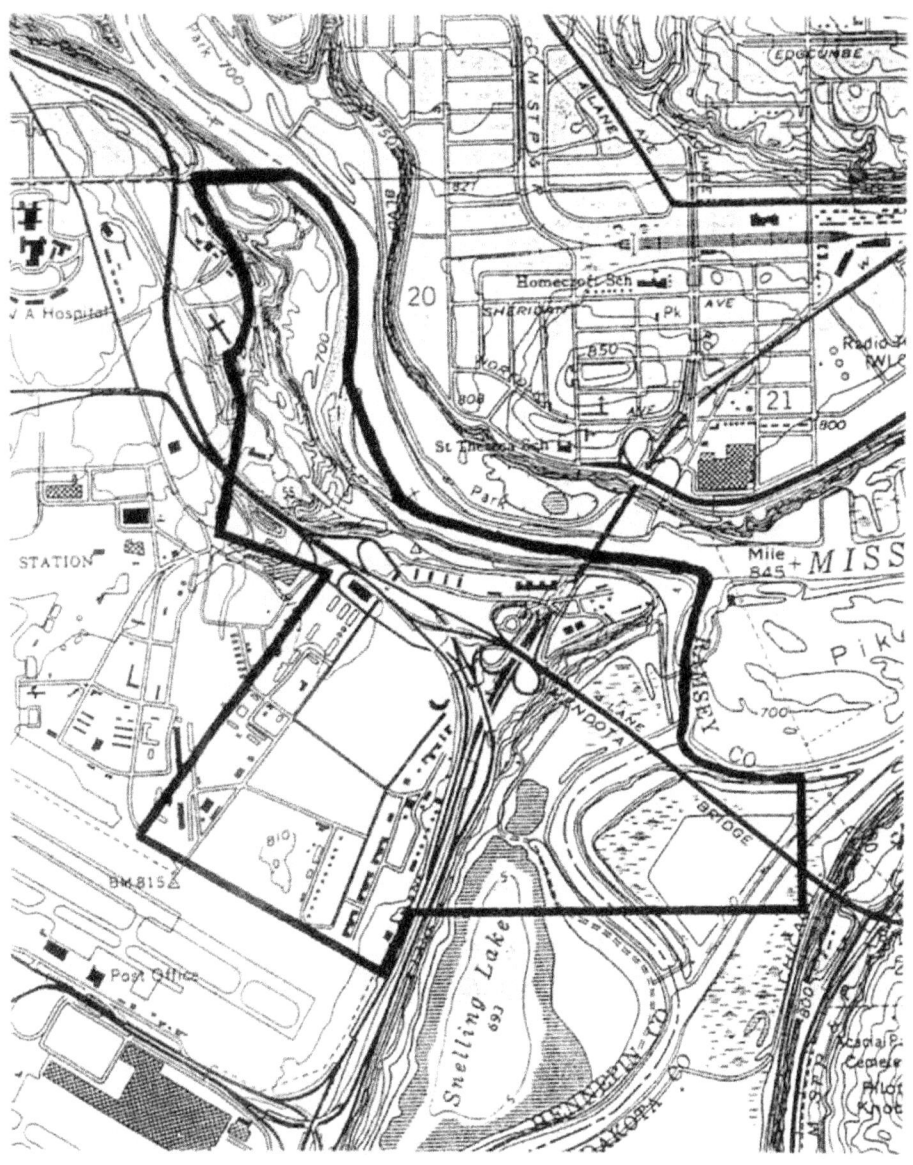

Figure 12. Fort Snelling National Register Historic District Boundaries

Figure 12

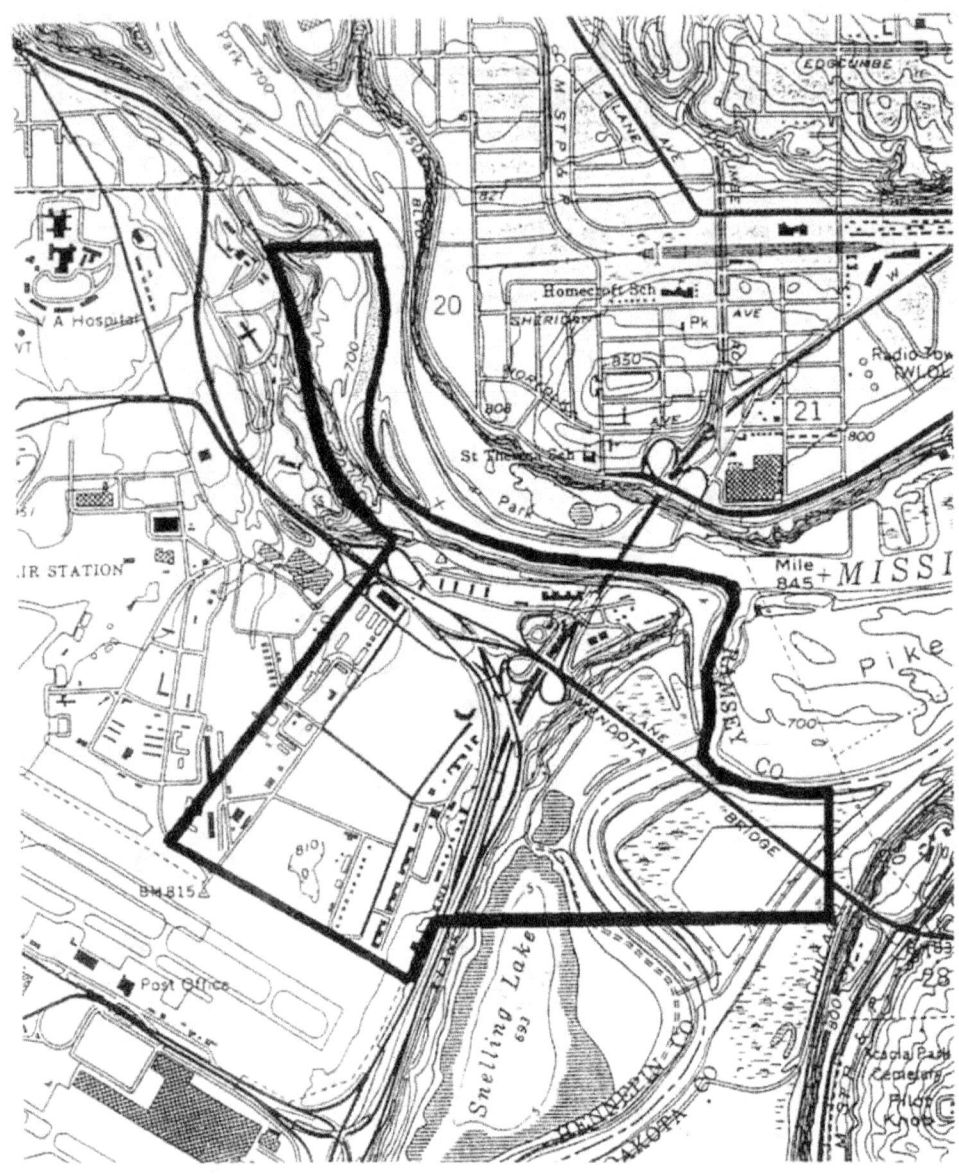

Figure 13. Old Fort Snelling (State) Historic District Boundaries

Figure 13

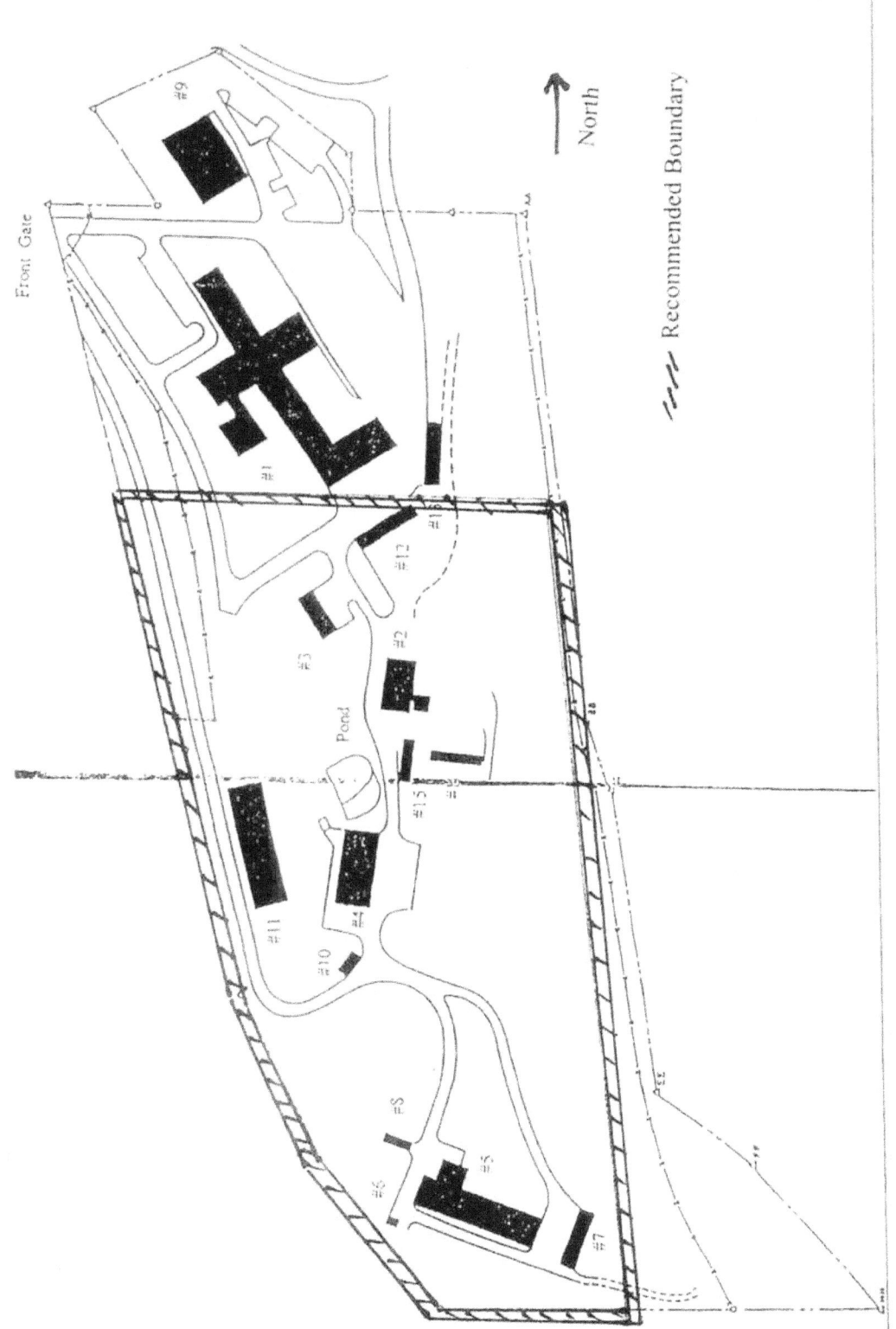

Figure 14. Recommended Boundary Changes Regarding Coldwater Spring Site at TCRC Property.

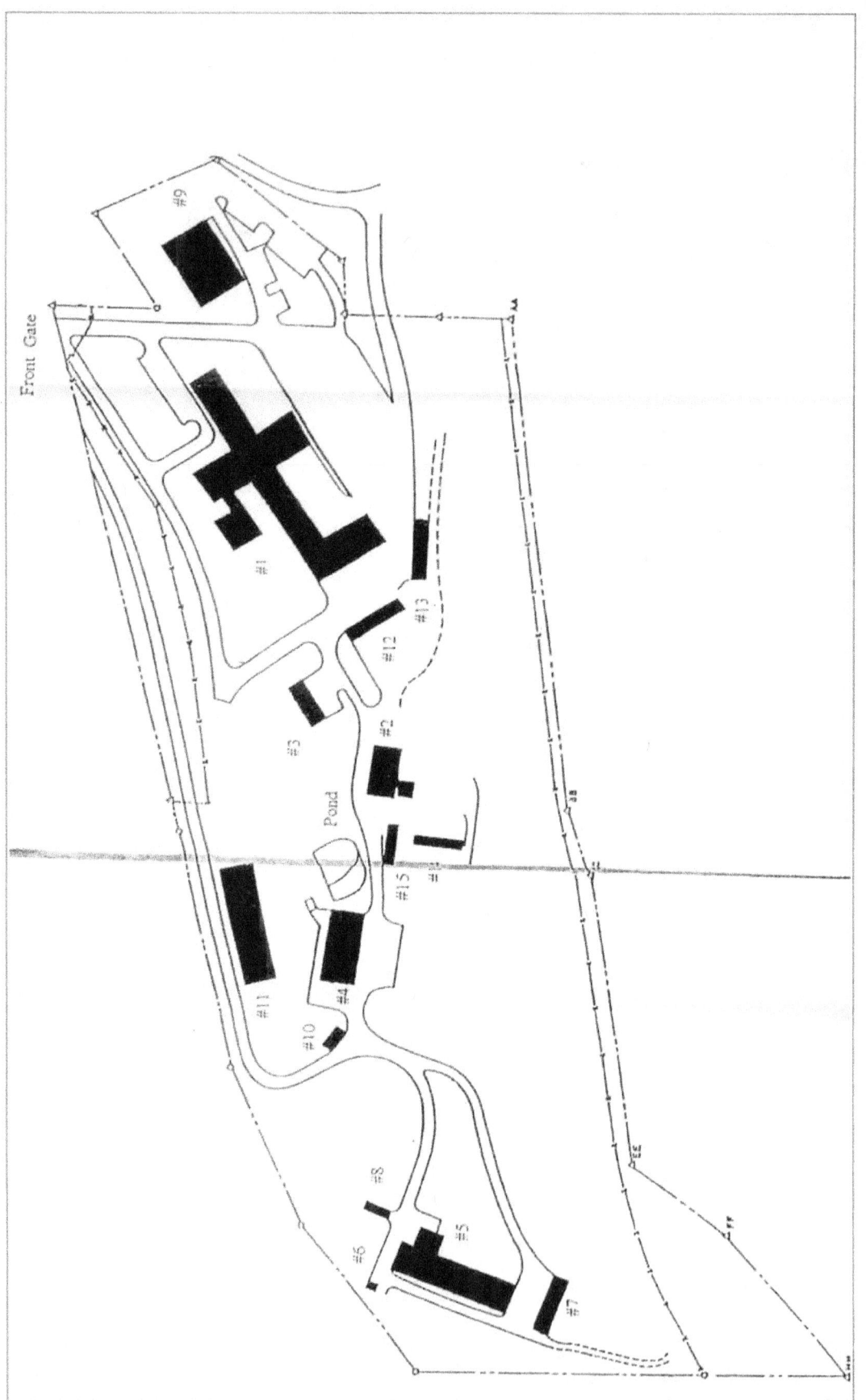

Figure 15. Proposed U.S. Bureau of Mines Twin Cities Research Center Historic District. Source: Ollendorf report, 1996.

Plate 1. Coldwater reservoir and spring house with possible George Lincoln farmstead in Background. Looking north.

Plate 2. Coldwater reservoir and spring house with pump house in background. Looking southwest. Ca. 1885. Source: MHS.

Plate 3. Brick engineer's quarters built at the Coldwater Spring waterworks in 1899.
Date of photograph not determined. Looking north? Source: MHS.

Plate 4. Coldwater Spring waterworks, including engineer's quarters, pump house, Reservoir, spring house, and two water tanks. Source: MHS.

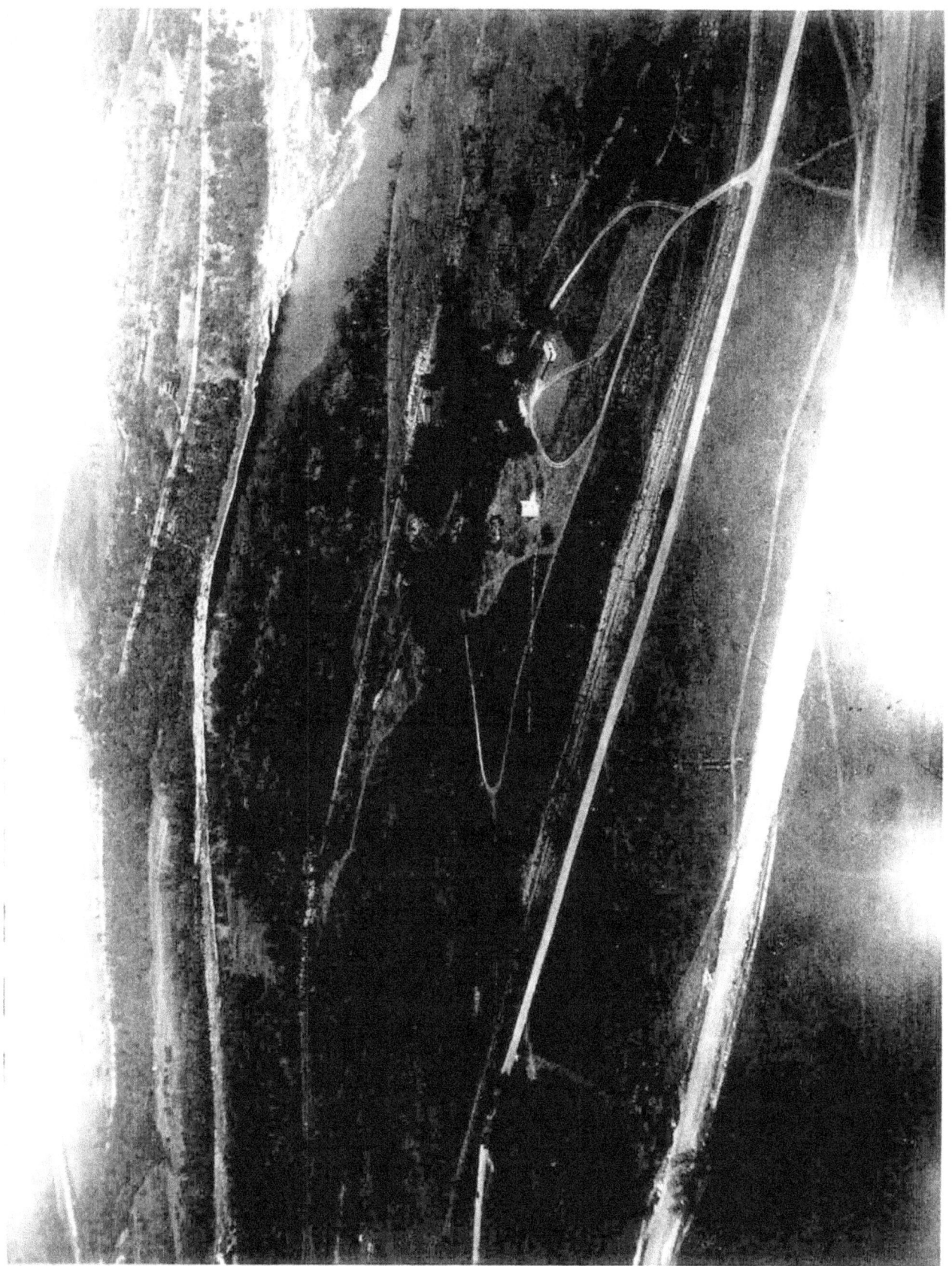

Plate 5. Aerial view of Coldwater Park. Ca. 1935. Source: MHS